THE WATER AND THE FIRE

The Water and the Fire

BY GERALD VANN O.P.

SHEED AND WARD NEW YORK

51900

NIHIL OBSTAT:
FR VICTOR WHITE, O.P., S.T.B.
FR CANICUS WYKEHAM-GEORGE, O.P., S.T.L

IMPRIMI POTEST:
FR HILARIUS CARPENTER, O.P.
PRIOR PROVINCIALIS
DIE 12 JANUARII 1953

NIHIL OBSTAT:
E. HARDWICK, CENSOR DEPUTATUS

IMPRIMATUR:
✠ LEO, EPUS. NORTHANTONIENSIS
DIE 3 FEBRUARII, 1953

BX
2350
V18
1954

Contents

I THE WORLD OF TOMORROW   *page* 7

II SOUND AND FURY: THE STILLNESS OF VISION   24

III EDUCATION: THE SEARCH FOR WISDOM   44

IV THE RECOVERY OF SYMBOL: THE HERO-KING   63

V THE RECOVERY OF SYMBOL: THE FIRE OF LIFE   80

VI THE RECOVERY OF SYMBOL: THE CHURCH'S
     DAILY LIFE   102

VII THE RECOVERY OF LOVE   117

VIII THE ROLE OF WOMAN   133

IX THE RECOVERY OF NATURE   145

X THE RECOVERY OF COMMUNITY   161

XI THE REDEMPTION OF MATTER   173

I

The World of Tomorrow

WHAT HUMAN life in any future age will be like there is of course no telling: humanity may find itself once again dwelling in the caves; for the matter of that, the caves themselves may have been 'vaporized.' But on the supposition that we shall be spared such major cataclysms, and that the world will go on much as it is going now, there is one thing we can do, and ought to do: we can examine contemporary trends of thought and behaviour, investigate the developing pattern of life as it is lived today by so many millions of human beings, and try to see just whither these things are leading and what may be done to alter what is evil in them.

That there is a great deal which is evil there can be no denying. All over the world the shoulders of men are bent with the crushing burdens of fear, of want, of miseries of one kind or another, of social injustice, of political tyranny. But beneath all these there is a deeper underlying evil: a psychological crisis through which humanity seems to be passing, and which threatens to destroy it more completely than any of these other things. There is something yet more menacing than the destruction of men's bodies, of their material environment, their comfort and security; and that is the voiding of the human spirit. One cannot blind oneself to the ugliness, the squalor, the cruelty, the stupidity, which seem more and more to darken human life today; but what lies so much deeper, and is so much more horrible, than these is the *unreality* of life today.

One aspect of this has been forcefully displayed in Gian-Carlo

7

Menotti's opera, *The Consul*, in which life and love and joy and sanity are destroyed, are smothered, by paper, by the ' forms ' without which nobody can live, nobody can move, nothing can be done, nothing can be achieved, and which yet are never obtainable—and at the end of the endless agony of waiting there is only death: the baby dies, the husband and wife cannot reach each other, there is only the utter emptiness of a telephone madly ringing to dead ears.

But political tyrannies, tensions, crises, or economic disasters, social upheavals: these at least are obvious and cannot fail to be noticed. What is so sinister is that the same need not at all be true of the underlying psychological changes; which go on slowly, inexorably, and may pass unnoticed until the damage is too complete to be remedied. That is why it is so important to try to understand now the way things are moving: now, while there is still so much vitality and awareness and hope left in human hearts. ' Where there is no vision, the people perish': and the people *are* perishing. The most urgent task in the world is to restore our vision in the time—the perhaps very short time—that is left us before it is too late, before the darkness closes in upon us.

One of the most obvious characteristics of life today in our modern technological world is the frenzied tempo at which that life has to be lived. Harassed people hurrying to business, hurrying from business, hurrying to snatch and gulp down a sandwich, hurrying to catch the overcrowded trains and buses, hurrying to jostle and be jostled through the subhumanity of rush-hour on the London Underground or—still worse—the New York Subway: these are ' types ' of twentieth-century humanity. And with the feverish speed and bustle of the modern city goes the appalling noise of the modern city: the scream and rattle and clangour of traffic and machinery. Many centuries ago, Boethius, living like ourselves at a world's end, steeled his soul against torture and death by turning his thoughts to the changeless tranquillity of the stars:

Aspice summi culmina caeli.
Illic iusto foedere rerum
Veterem seruant sidera pacem—

8

' Look to the highest of the heights of heaven,
See where the stars still keep their ancient peace ';[1]

for us, nowadays, even this ancient peace is shattered, if not by
the falling of fire from heaven, at least by the endless screaming
and roaring of jet-planes.

But we should be wrong to think of the noise and the frenzy
simply as something which modern man has to *suffer*: these things
are not only the cause, they are to some extent at least the effect,
of a deep underlying restlessness of spirit. A poet may cry,

' Teach us to sit still,'

but too often that is the last thing that modern man wants to learn
to do. A poet may sing of the

' sessions of sweet silent thought,'

but too often modern man will do anything to avoid silence,
because he finds thought, in any deep sense, very far from sweet.
Stillness, nowadays, tends to be regarded as a privation of movement, whereas in fact it is bustle and confusion which are a
privation of stillness. Silence, nowadays, tends to be regarded as
a privation of sound, whereas in fact it is noise which is a privation
of silence. So, all day long, the radio blares; all the time, whatever
is doing, there must be ' background music.' ' Silence,' writes
M. Max Picard, ' has been banished from the world today. All
that is left is muteness and emptiness. Silence seems to survive
only as a mere " structural fault " in the everlasting flow of noise.'[2]
But where there is no silence, no stillness, there can be no vision:
' In quiet and repose of the humours,' wrote Albertus Magnus
long ago, ' the soul attains understanding and prudence.' Without
that, we shall not learn: we shall not learn from the world around
us, from Nature, for ' the silent power of the landscape,' as M.
Picard remarks, ' needs the silence in the human face if it is to
exert its influence; ' we shall not learn from deep human relationships with other human beings and with all creatures, for ' ages

---

[1] *De Consolatione Philosophiae*, IV, 6; trans. Helen Waddell: *Wandering Scholars*, p. xxvi.
[2] Max Picard: *The World of Silence*, p. 92.

no longer related to silence, like the modern age, do not bother about the ontic in things. They are concerned only with the profitability, the exploitability, and the revolutionary possibilities in things;' we shall not learn from history, for such a world takes account only of the 'loud facts of history;' we shall not learn even from the fact of death, for even ' death itself has been killed,' has become ' merely something negative: the extreme end of what we call life.'[1]

The noise and the fever are in part the cause of our anxiety-ridden and neurotic restlessness; in part they are its effect. We have our share of complicity in creating the world we live in; for to a great extent the world we live in reflects and expresses the inner world of our own souls. There is tragic proof of this in the sphere of education. [The age-old idea of education as the quiet pursuit of wisdom, of fullness of life, of a rich, deep, completion of the whole personality, is disappearing; and is being replaced by a more and more exclusively utilitarian scramble to acquire knowledge of facts, and especially material facts, and above all, commercially rewarding facts. It is not merely that the personality as a whole is no longer engaged: the mind itself as a whole is no longer engaged. Wisdom must give way to efficiency; culture must give way to commerce. What is the use, people demand increasingly, of learning latin and greek? What is the use of all this poetry and music, this art and philosophy? *Utquid perditio haec*: Wherefore this waste? So Judas demanded as he watched the woman pouring out the precious ointment on the feet of God; and in his mean-minded calculation dismissed with a word all the poetry of life, all the poetry of holiness. And his words seem to be echoed down the ages in the mouths of all those who, in other contexts, have wanted to sell humanity's birthright for a mess of pottage. Wherefore this waste? Stupid parents of children of genius have cried through the centuries: Why not give up this silly scribbling of verses, this endless strumming on the piano, and find a good, steady, well-paid job? And more and more the same question is being repeated today: why not abolish all these useless things and be practical, concentrate on the things that will bring

[1] Picard, *op. cit.* pp. 106, 77, 84, 40.

in a good cash return? And of course if this view were ever to prevail universally it would mean that man would have lost practically everything that makes it worth while to be alive. It could be said with accuracy that the greatest and most urgent task of educators today is to instil ineradicably into the young precisely the utility of the useless, the value of the things that produce no cash returns but that make the 'soul worth saving.' 'A functionary,' writes Dr Josef Pieper, 'is trained. Training is defined as being concerned with some one side or aspect of man, with regard to some special subject. Education concerns the whole man; an educated man is a man with a point of view from which he takes in the whole world. Education concerns the whole man, man *capax universi*, capable of grasping the totality of existing things.' And he states the contemporary problem thus: 'Is it going to be possible to save men from becoming officials and functionaries and " workers " to the exclusion of all else? Can that possibly be done, and if so in what circumstances? There is no doubt of one thing: the world of the " worker " is taking shape with dynamic force—with such a velocity that, rightly or wrongly, one is tempted to speak of dæmonic force in history.'[1]

But this vulgarization, this destruction of educational ideals, is itself closely linked with, and no doubt dependent upon, a deeper loss: the loss of our roots in Nature. It is interesting and sad to note the immense difference of meaning which nowadays attaches to the two words (which etymologically are one word), urban and urbane. In other ages it was the urban population, the city dwellers, who were expected to be what we mean by urbane: polished, cultivated, courteous; while the rustic was expected to be uncouth and clownish. Nowadays, if you look for good manners, you are more likely to find them in the country lanes than in the market places of the cities; if you look for wisdom you are more likely to come across it in slow-witted country-people than in the slick racketeer who derides them. And perhaps the reason is that

---

[1] Josef Pieper: *Leisure the Basis of Culture*, pp. 45, 59. It should be noted that Dr Pieper is not using the term ' worker' as ' defining an occupation,' as ' synonymous with proletarian,' but ' in an anthropological sense' as implying 'a whole conception of " man " ' (cf. p. 29).

the *rusticus* still retains that deep contact with Nature, that rootedness in Nature, which the other has lost.

'The old Church,' wrote D. H. Lawrence, 'knew that life is here our portion, to be lived, to be lived in fulfilment. The stern rule of Benedict, the wild flights of Francis of Assisi, these were coruscations in the steady heaven of the Church. The rhythm of life itself was preserved by the Church, hour by hour, day by day, season by season, year by year, epoch by epoch, down among the people, and the wild coruscations were accommodated to this permanent rhythm. We feel it, in the south, in the country, when we hear the jangle of the bells at dawn, at noon, at sunset, marking the hours with the sound of mass or prayers. It is the rhythm of the daily sun. We feel it in the festivals, the processions, Christmas, the Three Kings, Easter, Pentecost, St John's Day, All Saints, All Souls. This is the wheeling of the year, the movement of the sun through solstice and equinox, the coming of the seasons, the going of the seasons. And it is the inward rhythm of man and and woman, too, the sadness of Lent, the delight of Easter, the wonder of Pentecost, the fires of St John, the candles on the graves of All Souls, the lit-up tree of Christmas, all representing kindled rhythmic emotions in the souls of men and women. . . . Oh, what a catastrophe for man when he cut himself off from the rhythm of the year, from his union with the sun and the earth. Oh, what a catastrophe, what a maiming of love when it was made a personal, merely personal feeling, taken away from the rising and setting of the sun, and cut off from the magic connection of the solstice and the equinox! This is what is the matter with us. We are bleeding at the roots, because we are cut off from the earth and sun and stars, and love is a grinning mockery, because, poor blossom, we plucked it from its stem on the tree of Life, and expected it to keep on blooming in our civilized vase on the table.'[1]

It is not only love that thus withers if it is torn away from its roots in Nature: it is man as a whole, body, mind and heart. It is not for nothing that the story of man begins in a garden. All through the ages men have learnt something, have learnt a great

[1] D. H. LAWRENCE: *Apropos of Lady Chatterley's Lover*, pp. 60-63.

deal, simply from their awareness of field and forest, of green and growing things, of birds and animals, of sun and moon and stars. Today there are masses of human beings to whom all this is denied. There are men and women who have been born and lived all their lives in some industrial slum; and who may never have known what it means to lie in the greenness of waving grasses, to watch the corn ripening under the summer sun; may never have listened to the chuckling of a brook, or known the smell of new-mown hay; never have watched a flight of birds on the wing, or listened to the voice of the forest; never have made anything with their hands out of nature's materials, a piece of wood, a block of stone; never even have seen the loaf coming hot and crisp from the oven, the wine pouring out from the wine-press. How immeasurably impoverished such a life must be: and what an appalling injustice that to such a life millions of men and women should be condemned by a social system!

Let it be added at once that there are others in far worse case than these: there are people who do live in contact with Nature, who are free to walk in field and forest, to listen to the voice of river or sea, but who in fact are blind and deaf to these things: having eyes they see not, and having ears they hear not, because psychologically speaking they are dead, and they are dead because, as we shall see, they have lost the faculty of wonder. For the moment we are concerned less with those who throw away their birthright than with those who are robbed of it. But in any case we have to recognize that, whatever one's particular setting and environment, the pattern of social life, the system, is such as to make us forget our roots in Nature unless we react very strenuously against it. We live in a cellophane age; more and more, things come to us at fourth or fifth remove from their natural state: the canned food and the canned music; the air-conditioned rooms and the potted ' reader's digest '; and life becomes more and more, in the strict sense, unnatural, and therefore more and more unreal.[1]

[1] Not of course that these things are not good and useful in themselves—even perhaps the digest—but there is something very wrong indeed with a society in which they wholly take the place of the natural condition of things. Wireless and gramophone are a wonderful consolation for those who cannot be present at the symphony concert; but they are not the equivalent of the concert.

The *system*. To concern oneself, as this first chapter must do, exclusively with what is 'wrong with the world' must inevitably seem a gloomy and graceless task unless all the time we bear in mind two things: first, that the vast mass of human beings are the victims of the system, rather than the wilful perpetrators of it; and secondly, that despite all the criticisms that can and must be levelled against the system, there is always the other side: the goodness and indeed the greatness of humanity is not quenched. The kindness, the shrewdness, the great-heartedness, the sheer *caritas*, which meet one at every turn: these continue to give the lie to any facile pessimism, and must put to shame any criticism which ignores them. But the more we appreciate the goodness of human beings, the more we must hate the evils of a system of life which victimizes them. It is in that sense that the 'evils' are enumerated in this chapter, to be discussed more constructively in the chapters which follow: we plunge into the darkness, our own darkness, only because of the promise of a renewal of light.

The loss of Nature is paralleled, and its ill effects are intensified, by the loss to so large an extent of all that the word 'home' has meant to mankind through the ages. The idea of marriage and family immediately implies that of home: house, garden, plot of land, in which and through which personalities could grow to their full stature, but which at the same time were the creation, the extension, of those same personalities. The family makes the home; the home helps to make the family. Nowadays, the stable setting, the fixed and perhaps traditional home, is often rendered impossible by the necessity of constant movement and removal; homes are broken up by divorce and re-marriage (and anyone who has been concerned in any way with children knows how often the neurotic or 'problem' child is the fruit of a broken home); but more than that, the very idea of home as something more than bricks and mortar, as a spiritual entity, as precisely the extension of the personalities concerned, seems to be disappearing. Le Corbusier defined a home as a 'machine for living in'; and while it is no doubt a useful definition from the point of view of the builder, from the psychological point of view it is, to say the least, extremely dangerous.

All through the ages the home has been both a reality of profound importance in its own right, and at the same time a symbol of profound significance. The walls are the symbol of the family's security from enemies and wild beasts without, and of its own unity within; the window is the symbol of vision, for the family must not be turned in upon itself but must look out upon the greater world, on the garden, the field, and thence to the wider, distant horizons, and in the end to the eternal hills; and the door is the symbol of that adventuring forth into life without which life can never be lived in its fullness, an adventuring which must somehow involve the sacrifice of security; and at the same time it is also the symbol of hospitality—the open door at which you welcome the friend or the stranger, and bid them come in and eat and drink and be warm. And be warm: the symbolism is only completed in the image of the hearth, the leaping flames, the crackle of the logs: it is round the hearth that the family gather in the evenings, to establish and deepen their love and their unity; it is to the hearth that you bring the traveller, to join the family circle. It is not without significance that in the world of today the hearth too, the open fire, is tending to disappear: all the benefits of central heating should not blind us to the fact that that there is something radically wrong when a family has nothing to gather around but the television, and when the best you can say to the traveller on your doorstep is, ' Come and warm yourself at my radiator.'

But this mention of the symbolism of the home takes us yet deeper into the heart of the matter. It is not only the loss of *this* symbolism we have to deplore; it is the loss of symbolism in general. Down through the ages humanity has learnt something at least, consciously or unconsciously, of the meaning of life through the great universal symbols as they come to him in myth and legend, in drama and folklore and fairy-tale. He has learnt something for instance of the meaning of the ' dark journey': the night-journey through forest or caverns or sea, wherein the hero must meet and conquer dragon or serpent or sorcerer, and in the end, out of the darkness, attain to rebirth, to fullness of life. For primitive man no doubt these things make up almost the whole of the psychological life, apart from the immediate necessities of every day; and in the great ages of civilization they still loom large, in art and poetry and drama, joining with philosophy and science to the creation of a rich and deep psychological life. But we for our part live in a lopsidedly cerebral age: the vast triumphs of science have caused us to neglect and perhaps to deride the other avenues to knowledge; we make use of symbols of course, but for the most part they are strictly practical and utilitarian, like the road signs or the barber's pole; the rest is largely lost. There are poets still, but few are interested to read them; there are artists still, but few are concerned to understand them; there are wise men, but few have time to listen to them.

So it is that here too in a very real sense we live in an unreal world: we have made science kill reality for us instead of illuminating it. We have verified in ourselves the old Hebrew proverb: In the mother's womb man knows the universe: at birth he forgets it. Lawrence spoke wisely again, within his limitations, when he wrote: 'The universe is dead for us, and how is it to come to life again? " Knowledge " has killed the sun, making it a ball of gas, with spots; " knowledge " has killed the moon, it is a little dead earth fretted with extinct craters as with smallpox; the machine has killed the earth for us, making it a surface, more or less bumpy, that you travel over;' and the vastness and splendour of the triumphs of science should not blind us to the yet greater importance of what we are in danger of losing, the other sort of knowledge— 'the purring of the great gold lion of the sun, who licks us like a lioness her cubs, making us bold, or else, like the red, angry lion, dashes at us with open claws;'—should not blind us to the fact that 'we are perishing for lack of fulfilment of our greater needs, we are cut off from the great sources of our inward nourishment and renewal, sources which flow eternally in the universe. Vitally, the human race is dying. It is like a great uprooted tree, with its roots in the air. We must plant ourselves again in the universe.'[1]

To put all this in other terms: the modern world tends to reduce the life of the mind more and more exclusively to the use of reason, especially in its scientific and practical aspects, and to ignore or stifle the other functions of the psyche: sense, feeling,

[1] D. H. Lawrence, *op. cit.* pp. 86, 88, 83.

intuition. And it is tempting to see this state of affairs as due in part to another modern phenomenon: the loss to greater or less extent of the vocation of woman as such. The battle for the emancipation of women was of course, in essentials, quite simply a struggle to right a wrong, to give women at long last the elementary human rights which were their due. But there seems to have been at times a confusion between equality of rights and equality *tout court*, so that the securing of equal rights, equal dignity, for both sexes turned in fact too often into a levelling away of all differences between the sexes. (Thus the securing in education of equal rights for women seems to have resulted sometimes in a slavish imitation of the type of education proper to men rather than in the creation of a type of education proper to women.) The tendency to equalization was no doubt given further impetus by the demands of the two world wars, which imposed upon women many of the tasks—and to that extent the modes of thought—of men. To this in its turn is no doubt largely attributable the degree in which other differences between the two sexes have been minimized—in dress, manners, vocabulary, and so forth. But if this is so, if these more superficial assimilations mean that at a deep psychological level the differences are being levelled out also, it must signify an immense impoverishment of life for man and woman alike. For the whole point of the differences is that they are complementary.

It is of course impossible to generalize. Nobody is psychologically speaking one hundred per cent male or female. There are many women whose clear vocation it is, as individuals, to make a career for themselves in the world, to be artists, poets, politicians, surgeons, and so on. What can be said, however, is that when all due allowance has been made for individual differences and vocations, it remains true that on the whole the minds of man and woman as such tend to work differently: his with the emphasis on the rational, hers on the intuitive; and that it is this very difference which makes them complement each other, correct and enrich each other, and so, in love and marriage, makes the total human entity, the unity of the two in one, something so much richer and deeper than they could ever be in isolation. If woman, then, neglects or loses her own particular birthright, both man and woman suffer, the whole human race suffers. And as it is to the non-rational functions of the mind that symbols appeal, it could be woman's particular office, and glory, to lead humanity back through symbolism to a saner and fuller psychological life—but that she cannot do if she herself has lost her own understanding of them.

There is something more. Woman is closer to nature, to the material world, than man; and to that extent she should be in a special sense the guardian—and the restorer—of the dignity of matter and of the material world. Yet today we are witnessing the tragedy of a degradation of matter on a scale hitherto unknown. You think of the way in which torture or drugs are used today not just to destroy men's bodies but to destroy their personalities; you think of the appalling degradation—and on how appallingly vast a scale—of concentration camps and gas-chambers. But behind all this there is the much more widespread, the almost universal, loss of reverence for all material things. In the words of M. Picard already quoted, the modern world is concerned 'only with the profitability, the exploitability, and the revolutionary possibilities in things.' Just as men are treated as mere 'hands,' 'units,' numbers on a form, so things are treated as mere utilities: we see God's creatures and make use of them, we do not stop to look at them, to learn them and love them for themselves. What an abyss separates us from the Russian *Staretz* who would not have his disciples idly, wantonly, pluck even a leaf from a tree or destroy a blade of grass! And where the works not of God's hands but of man's are concerned, it is humbling to reflect that we keep in our museums and art galleries the ordinary household utensils, the pots and pans, of other civilizations, and indeed of our own fore-bears, not merely because they are of historical interest but because they are beautiful: our own domestic wares may perhaps find their way eventually into museums, it is hardly likely that the bulk of them will ever see the inside of an art gallery. We get the goods we deserve. We degrade matter and treat it irreverently; and so in our turn we are degraded by matter.

All day long we are seeing things but we never find time to

18

stop and look and wonder at them: to be still, and concentrate our gaze on them until they begin to reveal their secrets to us, the mystery which lies within them. We never stop to look, and so the beauty of things passes us by; equally, we never stop to look and so we fail to notice all the ugliness and squalor with which we surround ourselves. Wonder is one of the faculties most easy to lose: we have it in childhood, undiscriminating no doubt but vivid and deep; we all too easily lose it as we grow older and become immersed in our daily concerns; and so, unless we are very careful, not beauty only but life itself passes us by. For inevitably life loses its meaning when it loses its mystery. Take the mystery out of love and it ceases to be love and becomes merely a biochemical equation; take the mystery out of art and it becomes the mindless daubs or the commercialized sex you find on hoardings or in magazines. Take the mystery out of the blade of grass, the leaf, the petal of the flower, and you might just as well be blind for you will never see the secret heart of things, you might just as well be deaf for you will never hear the song of the spheres.

'Where there is no vision the people perish;' but in the world of today there is less and less vision because it becomes increasingly more and more activist, more and more remote from awareness, from contemplation. 'Nature herself,' wrote Evelyn Underhill, 'reveals little of her secret to those who only look and listen with the outward ear and eye. The condition of all valid seeing and hearing, upon every plane of consciousness, lies not in the sharpening of the senses, but in a peculiar attitude of the whole personality: in a self-forgetting attentiveness, a profound concentration, a self-merging, which operates a real communion between the seer and the seen—in a word, in *contemplation*.'[1]

If we may for the moment tentatively define contemplation in this wide sense as a loving awareness, it would seem indeed that the ultimate cause of all our troubles is the lack of it. 'We begin,' writes Mr. Aldous Huxley, 'by lacking charity towards Nature, so that instead of trying to co-operate with Tao or the Logos on the inanimate and sub-human levels, we try to dominate and exploit, we waste the earth's mineral resources, ruin its soil, ravage

---

[1] Evelyn Underhill: *Mysticism* (14th edit. 1942), p. 300.

its forests, pour filth into its rivers and poisonous fumes into its air. From lovelessness in relation to Nature we advance to lovelessness in relation to art—a lovelessness so extreme that we have effectively killed all the fundamental or useful arts and set up various kinds of mass-production by machines in their place. And of course this lovelessness in regard to art is at the same time a lovelessness in regard to the human beings who have to perform the fool-proof and grace-proof tasks imposed by our mechanical art-surrogates and by the interminable paper work connected with mass-production and mass-distribution. With mass-production and mass-distribution go mass-financing, and the three have conspired to expropriate ever-increasing numbers of small owners of land and productive equipment, thus reducing the sum of freedom among the majority and increasing the power of a minority to exercise a coercive control over the lives of their fellows. This coercive controlling minority is composed of private capitalists or governmental bureaucrats or of both classes of bosses acting in collaboration—and, of course, the coercive and therefore essentially loveless nature of the control remains the same, whether the bosses call themselves " company directors " or " civil servants ".'[1]

Loneliness may indeed be one of the demons who stalk most arrogantly through our vast overcrowded centres of population. Too often the modern city-dweller must pass his life (apart from moments of common danger and crisis: you can find real brotherhood in an air-raid shelter) oscillating uneasily between the two extremes of loneliness and mass hysteria: loneliness as he goes about the business of earning his daily bread, mass hysteria in the rare moments when he finds himself provided with circuses. In former ages the social organism was far more articulated, the boundaries of the various classes and strata far more rigidly defined, than today; and yet you find an equally obvious common bond, a common life, a common interest. It is very clear in Chaucer; it is very clear in Fielding. It is still to be found in village life—in *The Little World of Don Camillo*, for instance, where the catholic priest and the communist mayor are officially enemies but are secretly devoted to each other; or in those French films which

[1] Aldous Huxley: *The Perennial Philosophy*, pp. 109-110

depict so admirably the feuds and battles of village life (the *bien-pensants*, the anti-clericals) under which however you discern unmistakably the unity of a real family life. But in the vast amorphous modern town it is all gone: there is organization but no organic life; centralization, bureaucracy have killed personal initiative and, just as surely, the atomization of society into vast agglomerations of ' units ' has killed personalism. All the time, in shops and offices, in trains and buses and cinemas and restaurants, people are dealing with other human beings—but they may not notice they are human beings. They may not even know who their next-door neighbours are: which is presumably the same as saying that they are not their neighbours in the Gospel sense at all. Their daily lives are largely regimented by officials whom they do not know, and who for their part are far less interested in them as persons than in the tidiness—or sometimes, one fears, the sheer complexity—of their forms and blue-prints. But a life from which personal relationships and a natural, lively interest in people, are excluded is a radically unhealthy life. It is an unreal life.

It must be repeated that all this is but one side of the picture. There is still far too much kindness and greatness in human nature, far too much common sense, far too much creativeness, far too much wisdom, above all, far too much real charity in human beings to allow of their being swamped by the system under which they live, the unreality of the world in which they live. But that does not alter the fact that the system is so largely evil, the world they live in is so largely unreal. It does not alter the fact that a world such as that cannot endure. It must either end in complete destruction, or it must undergo a radical change.[1]

Mankind's first sin was pride of intellect; and today it seems as though that sin had at last all but completed the circle of evil, and brought humanity from the first act of self-creation in counterfeit grandeur to a final act of self-destruction. Intellect, in the pride of its scientific achievements, docketed reality, denying the validity of anything which refused to be subject to this treatment, and so robbed humanity not only of religion but even of poetry, even of

---

[1] The next five paragraphs are adapted from an article, *Retreat into Reality*, published in *Blackfriars*, July-Aug. 1951.

earthly vision; it subjugated everything to the successful search for power, till man himself became the threatened victim of the power; it killed the instinctive and intuitive life which could give man happiness and richness in spite of much material misery; it led him away from the nothingness which is the womb out of which mysticism creates life to the nothingness in which nihilism seeks death.

' If,' writes Professor Guitton, ' the culture which we have cherished through so many centuries of labour and leisure is to have a chance of survival it is because, in the midst of it (and, in a sense, in spite of it) we shall see the emergence of a type of mind which will accept existence, employing the power of pure mind to rediscover and justify precisely that which mind, when pure, is tempted to dissolve. But a real conversion will be required, a radical reversal of mind, that the dimensions of being may thus be rediscovered.'[1]

The first sin in man's history was the proud determination to dominate; and now we have dominated to such purpose that we can and perhaps will destroy everything, including ourselves. If we think of love as domination we shall never know love; if we think of morality as domination, as a self-achieved self-mastery, we shall never know holiness; if we think of progress as the domination of Nature we shall never know happiness. Intellect—scientific, analytical, practical—has been abused, has been developed and idolized at the expense of the psyche as a whole; if we are to return to sanity it must be through the return of intellect to its fundamental purposes, to wonder, adoration, vision, wisdom, all of which can spring only from humility and *inwardness*.

When we are young the physical world, material things, bodily activity, may absorb us; when we grow old these things may be withdrawn from us: activity an effort instead of a joy, the material world dimmed, the zest for living departed. It is then that if we have no inner kingdom to repair to we feel upon us the cold hand of despair: there is nothing left but unrelieved boredom, a negative waiting for death. It is life itself which teaches us that growth is an inward thing; that if existence is not to become thinner and thinner

[1] Jean Guitton: *Essay on Human Love*, p. 220.

till it reaches sheer meaninglessness we must discover the inner world, which is also the greater world in which the universe is but a speck, wherein our knowledge and love of the earth may be rekindled and deepened as, long ago in so different a way, they were kindled and coloured by our first experience of love. In youth we tend to go out to life, to conquer it; later we realize that what we needed above all was to learn to sit still, to beg life to come to us and take possession of us.

The experience of the race repeats the experience of the individual. The young races go out to war; they conquer the effete civilizations; in their turn they become a civilization; it is then that they must turn inward if they are not to suffer the fate of those they conquered. But what is more difficult than such a change of heart? And we for our part, we have become so 'cerebral' that we have cut ourselves off from our roots in the universe and in God. There is nothing we can do about it except to re-learn, consciously, what we have lost, in the hope of then making it gradually not just something we have learnt but something we have lived. It is on that quest for inwardness that everything now depends.

These characteristics, then, of modern technological society which we have been considering—the frenzied tempo, the disintegration of education, the loss of our roots in Nature and in home life, the loss of symbols, of the vocation of woman, of organic community life, the degradation of matter—these are far from being unrelated. They are, on the contrary, manifestations of one central fact: an impoverishment of the human spirit which goes very deep indeed and which seems likely, unless something is done, to lead to a final eclipse of the spirit in the life of our society. It will be the concern of the following chapters to examine these various characteristics more in detail; and to see what might be done to remedy the situation before it is too late.

II

Sound and Fury: The Stillness of Vision

AMONG THE qualities which seem particularly to characterize life today we began by considering the noise and the bustle of the modern city: the frenzied tempo at which life is lived, the multiplicity of pursuits and concerns, the atmosphere of ceaseless hurry; and at the same time the sheer din in the midst of which all that is doing has to be done. There is no time to think, to ask the ultimate questions of why and whither; but even if there were time it would be difficult to think in the midst of the jangling of machinery and the screaming of jet-planes.

But we should be taking a very superficial view of the state of affairs if we thought of the noise as being exclusively or even primarily a question of physical noise. With sufficient knowledge, courage and training it is possible to abstract from physical noise as it is possible to abstract from physical pain. It is said of St Thomas Aquinas that when he had to undergo considerable pain at the hands of the surgeon he immersed himself in deep speculation and became oblivious of what was being done to him; he achieved much the same result, less wittingly, when his preoccupation with the problem of manicheism plunged him into a brown study at the no doubt sufficiently noisy banqueting table of the King of France. But there are other kinds of noise which are more insistent.

'The twentieth century,' writes Mr Aldous Huxley, 'is, among other things, the Age of Noise. Physical noise, mental noise and noise of desire—we hold history's record for all of them.

And no wonder: for all the resources of our almost miraculous technology have been thrown into the current assault against silence. That most popular and influential of all recent inventions, the radio, is nothing but a conduit through which pre-fabricated din can flow into our homes.[1] And this din goes far deeper, of course, than the ear-drums. It penetrates the mind, filling it with a babel of distractions—news items, mutually irrelevant bits of information, blasts of corybantic or sentimental music, continually repeated doses of drama that bring no catharsis, but merely create a craving for daily or even hourly emotional enemas. And where, as in most countries, the broadcasting stations support themselves by selling time to advertisers, the noise is carried from the ears, through the realms of phantasy, knowledge and feeling to the ego's central core of wish and desire. Spoken or printed, broadcast over the ether or on woodpulp, all advertising copy has but one purpose—to prevent the will from ever achieving silence. Desire-lessness is the condition of deliverance and illumination. The condition of an expanding and technologically progressive system of mass-production is universal craving. Advertising is the organized effort to extend and intensify craving—to extend and intensify, that is to say, the workings of that force which (as all the saints and teachers of all the higher religions have always taught) is the principal cause of suffering and wrong-doing and the greatest obstacle between the human soul and its divine Ground.'[2]

The modern world is killing leisure. True, the working hours grow shorter and shorter; we approach perhaps what is sometimes called the 'leisure State'; yet in fact what is left when work is over is all too often not leisure at all but (at best) inactivity. Offices,

[1] This may well seem a far too sweeping stricture on broadcasting in general and perhaps on the painstaking labours of the B.B.C. in particular. Given a certain critical sense, the wireless can be indeed an inestimable boon: it can bring one music and drama to which otherwise one would not have access; it can bring one views and discussions in which one is interested and which one wants to hear. And yet, to find oneself for instance laid up in bed with nothing to do but listen to the wireless all day long is a sombre experience. There is seldom anything—apart perhaps from half an hour's music or so—pleasant or perhaps even bearable to listen to in the mornings, musical or otherwise; and yet in fact—and it is with facts that we are concerned—all over the country the wireless sets blare away, from dawn to dewy eve: they are precisely no more than conduits ' through which pre-fabricated din ' not only can but does, relentlessly, remorselessly, flow into our homes. Given a critical sense it would be different, yes; but where is the critical sense?

[2] Huxley: *op. cit.* pp. 249-250.

shops and factories close; but the noise goes on, the frenzy goes on, the wireless blares, the cinemas and other purveyors of passive amusement fill up. Passive amusement in general, and films in particular (if they are good ones), are good things in themselves, but they are not what western civilization has meant by leisure, which is a creative thing.

'One of the foundations of western culture,' writes Dr Pieper, 'is leisure. That much, at least, can be learnt from the first chapter of Aristotle's *Metaphysics*. And even the history of the word attests the fact: for leisure in Greek is *skole*, and in Latin *schola*, the English 'school.' The word used to designate the place where we educate and teach is derived from a word which means leisure.'[1]

Leisure, in other words, creative leisure, is the condition of knowledge: 'be still, and know.' It is the condition of vision. Such an idea, however, is the exact contrary of a view currently held at the present day concerning the pursuit of knowledge. Dr Pieper goes on to quote the aristotelean maxim that 'we work in order to have leisure;' and points out how this in its turn is the opposite of an accepted view that on the contrary 'we live to work' and that any other theory 'sounds immoral, as though directed at the very foundations of human society.'[2]

Here indeed we must make a distinction. In the ideal condition of things, a man's work is his vocation, and it is that therefore, in a real sense, for which he lives; the more so as it is (again in the ideal condition of things) a creative work, since 'the artist is not a special kind of man, but every man is a special kind of artist.' But it remains true that real creative activity can only be the outcome of contemplation, and therefore of leisure: the artist will defeat his own ends unless he has the leisure to achieve his own particular form of vision; and therefore it remains true that while in one sense he lives to work, in another sense he works in order to have leisure.

It is important to make this distinction clear because it is important to re-instate the ideal of work as creative activity instead of the uncreative but commercially-rewarding 'job.' At the same time it is equally important to combat the idea of what Dr Pieper

[1] Pieper, *op. cit.* pp. 25-26.   [2] *op. cit.* p. 26.

calls 'the world of "total work"' or 'planned diligence.' This idea, as he points out, affects not only the sphere of manual labour but that of intellectual labour as well; for it means that knowledge is thought of as 'exclusively an active, discursive labour of the *ratio*, the reason.' 'Look at the "worker",' he writes again, 'and you will see that his face is marked by strain and tension, and these are even more pronounced in the case of the "intellectual worker." These are the marks of that perpetual activity (exclusive of all else) of which Goethe remarked that "it ends in bankruptcy." They are the revealing marks of the intellectual sclerosis that comes with not being able to receive or accept, of that hardening of the heart that refuses to suffer anything; and in their extreme form such tensions become vocal in the lunatic assertion "every action has some meaning, even a crime; but to be passive is always senseless." '[1]

Vacate et videte: 'Be at leisure and *see* that I am the Lord': how far we have moved from this traditional, this secular, view of the way to wisdom! 'While all things were in quiet silence,' we read in the *Book of Wisdom*, 'and that night was in the midst of her swift course, Thine Almighty Word, O Lord, leapt down out of thy Royal Throne';[2] and again in the book of the *Apocalypse*, in two verses which the Breviary unites: 'There was silence in heaven while the dragon fought against Michael the Archangel.'[3] So it was too that when Elias looked for the Lord he found him, not in the mighty wind, the fire, the earthquake, but in the sound of the still, small voice, or, as the Vulgate has it, the whisper of a gentle wind.[4] So it is that the great teachers have always insisted that vision will be achieved only if the search begins in silence and stillness.

'The idea of stillness, unity and peace,' wrote Evelyn Underhill, 'is and has ever been humanity's best translation of its intuition of the achieved Perfection of God. "'In the midst of silence a hidden word was spoken to me.' Where is this Silence, and where is the place in which this word is spoken? It is in the purest that the soul can produce, in her noblest part, in the Ground, even the Being of the Soul." So Eckhart: and here he does but subscribe to a universal tradition. The mystics have always insisted that " Be

---

[1] *op. cit.* pp. 36-37.   [2] xviii, 14-15.   [3] viii, 1; xii, 7.   [4] III Kings, xix, 11-13.

still, be still, and *know* " is the condition of man's purest and most direct apprehensions of reality: that he experiences in quiet the truest and deepest activity: and christianity when she formulated her philosophy made haste to adopt and express this paradox.'[1]

'He who knows,' said Lao Tzu, 'does not speak; he who speaks does not know.' And the Mundaka Upanishad: 'What is above creation cannot be attained by action . . . To a pupil who comes with mind and senses in peace the Teacher gives the vision of Brahman, of the Spirit of truth and eternity.'

How has the modern world come to reverse so completely these universally accepted values? How has it come to be so *activist*? How did it lose the idea of the life of mind as essentially a *theoria*: a search for vision, for wisdom, a 'listening,' in Heraclitus' phrase, 'to the essences of things'? No doubt we must look for the answer to those historical processes which led to an ever greater and more exclusive emphasis being laid on one of the four functions of the psyche to the relative neglect of the rest: on reason as opposed to intuition, senses, feeling, and, in the last resort, on practical scientific reason to the exclusion of everything else. Descartes, brooding over his stove and deciding that the purpose of metaphysics is to secure for man the mastery of Nature, is a symbol of the whole sorry process.

And sorry it is; not of course on its positive side, the immense (and, to other ages, all but unimaginable) triumphs of scientific investigation, but on its negative side, its warping of the personality (about which the psychologists have plenty to tell us) and its impoverishment of humanity as a whole. Quite apart from all that the loss of religious faith and insight has meant to modern man, even in the most strictly human and humanist terms, we have to reckon with the loss to the common man, to all intents and purposes, of all that poetry, drama, art, music, myth and symbol, ritual and ceremonial, have meant to men through the ages; and we have to reckon with the fact that, because of the loss of the idea of *theoria*, because of his activist attitude to reality, he is in danger not only of never finding life in its fullness, but also of developing in himself that which most inevitably leads to ugliness, to cruelty

[1] Underhill, *Mysticism*, p. 38.

and brutality, to greed and the glorifying of all the predatory instincts.

For what, in the end, does activism mean? It means thinking of knowledge in terms of possessing truth, possessing power, possessing the mastery of Nature; it means thinking of life in terms of possessing the means to pleasure or profit or power, to mastery and domination; it means thinking of love in terms of possessing something or somebody. But this is something very like the original sin: Ye shall be as gods—deciding for yourselves what shall be good and what shall be evil: ye shall be as gods, dominating and domineering over the rest of creation: ye shall be as gods, not accepting truth from elsewhere but making your own truth. ' What is above creation cannot be attained by action ': and in the last resort the same is true of creation itself. Knowledge, love, life: these all issue in action, no doubt; but if the action is to be wise and beneficent it must be the fruit of contemplation. And they do, no doubt, in a sense mean possession: but only if the possession *of* is a part—and a humble part—of possession *by*. To possess we must first learn to be possessed: because life, first of all and essentially, means being possessed *by* reality, letting reality flood into the heart and the soul; and love means being possessed *by* love, living in love, as Dante, when Beatrice met him in the street, ' was so highly moved that he was, for the moment, in a state of complete good-will, complete *caritas* towards everyone ';[1] and wisdom in its turn (as opposed to mere cleverness, or learning, or the kind of knowledge which, as St Paul says, ' puffeth up ') means being possessed *by* truth, laying open the mind and heart to reality, ' listening to the essences of things,' being contemplative, being receptive, and so coming in the end to be a seer.

The soul is feminine to God. An activist world is a world which thinks it can be masculine to reality without first being feminine. It cannot. Gender is a much wider term than sex: whether human beings are male or female they have to learn the same essential lesson: that they must be feminine before they can hope with success to be masculine: they must be contemplative before they can hope to be wisely and graciously active: they

---

[1] Charles Williams: *Religion and Love in Dante*, p. 9.

must receive before they attempt to give. The great scientists know this, who humbly sit at the feet of reality before they attempt to use the resources of reality; the great philosophers know it, who will not attempt to imprison reality with all its mysteries into a neat and finite system; the poets and artists and makers of music know it, who give the world only what they have heard or seen; the wise men know it, who when they have made as best they can their explanation of reality, realize humbly that their best is merely ' as so much straw.'

But we lose the vision—we lose even the possibility of the vision—if we lose the sense of mystery; and we lose the sense of mystery when we lose the sense of wonder. Yet that is precisely what, to so large an extent, we have done. Dr Pieper, reminding us how St Thomas notes in his commentary on the *Metaphysics* of Aristotle that ' the philosopher is related to the poet in that both are concerned with *mirandum*, with wonder, with marvelling and that which makes us marvel,' goes on to point out that ' our sense of wonder, in the philosophical meaning of the word, is not aroused by enormous, sensational things—though that is what a dulled sensibility requires to provoke it to a sort of *ersatz* experience of wonder. A man who needs the unusual to make him " wonder " shows that he has lost the capacity to find the true answer to the wonder of being.' For indeed, ' the beginning of philosophy ' is ' to perceive all that is unusual and exceptional, all that is wonderful, in the midst of the ordinary things of everyday life.'[1]

The ordinary things: the human beings, animals, sun and moon and stars, day and night, the earth and its fullness

' *My heart leaps up when I behold* '—

that is the beginning of poetry and philosophy alike. Where human beings are concerned, the Church gives us a striking lesson

---

[1] Pieper, *op. cit.* pp. 95, 131-2. We might compare with this some lines of Clive Bell on Proust: ' For him nothing was intrinsically insignificant . . . He observed banalities after the manner of his beloved Impressionists, staring at familiar objects till they gave up their secrets, till he had penetrated the dust and dirt of familiarity and discovered underneath that thrilling reality which is the thing itself.' And he added: ' As Proust knew, there are drugs: for the common man the common round, the daily task, a little golf, a good deal of whisky, regular unemotional sensuality at fixed intervals, leading on to premature imbecility and an unearned grave. The normal man escapes from life by never living intensely.' (Clive Bell: *Proust*, pp. 62, 86.)

in the marriage ritual, where the man is to say to the woman: With my body I thee worship.[1] They are to approach each other with love, understanding, desire, passion, pity, joy; but underneath all this there must be wonder and reverence because a human being is a mystery which must be learnt slowly, lovingly, with care and tenderness and pain, and which is never learnt completely. 'The beginning of wisdom is the fear—awe, reverence—of the Lord,' we are told; without wonder and reverence we shall never learn the secret heart of things.

There is an interesting side-light on all this to be found in the works of the great French novelist, M. Francois Mauriac, who is often accused by his critics of being guilty of a kind of Jansenism.[2] Why is it that in the novels of Mauriac there seem to be no *happy* love-stories? It is not that he does not know what the glory can be; on the contrary. 'Where his mother had made a mistake,' he writes in one of the novels, 'was in not realizing that the body, too, can be sanctified. A young man and a young girl blaze in the face of God like two high clear flames. Drawn into one another, they shine the brighter.' None the less, the loves he himself portrays are painted in sombre colours; and the reason seems to be clear enough. He is very concerned—one might almost say obsessed— with the ' animality ' of human love: with its cruelty and egoism; with the inequality of the love of any two lovers for each other; with the difference between the idealized picture of the beloved object and the reality; with the idea that love is essentially a *lutte*, a battle, and that it is inescapably sterile since in the last resort we can never really succeed in *knowing* anyone else.

Now all these things are true, in fact, not of love but of sex in isolation from love. It is sex in isolation that is animal, cruel, selfish, unreal, sterile; but when it is really human—when, that is, it is an element in a total, shared, psycho-physical love and union —then happiness is indeed possible. For the concern of the lovers is then precisely to make flesh the vehicle of spirit: to achieve through physical passion the union of the two personalities, two minds and two hearts; to infuse animality with tenderness; to

---

[1] Cf. *infra*, ch. VII.
[2] I adapt here some pages from my essay on *The Problem of the Catholic Novelist*, published in the Walter Farrell Memorial Volume of *The Thomist*, 1952, *from an Abundant Spring*.

overcome inequality; to learn to love this real person and not some idealized self-projection; to conquer selfishness and turn the isolated pursuit of pleasure into a sharing of a common joy and a mutual discovery. It is the concern of the man to temper his male sex-aggressiveness by saying and living the words already quoted, With my body I thee worship. It is for both of them to achieve this humanizing of sex and, what is more, to raise it from a humanly lovely to a divinely lovely thing by learning together to make their love of each other a way to and an expression of their love of reality: of the earth, of the human family, of God.

Why then is Mauriac's picture so remote from this human reality? It is tempting to see the answer in a colouring of his thought by that very activism we have been considering, so that he sees love, of man and of God alike, as desire to possess or joy in possessing.

The Holy Eucharist, he tells us, means 'possessing what one loves.' But in the last resort it does not: it means exactly the opposite: it means being possessed by what one loves, or what one tries ineffectually to love. Human love in its turn of course includes the desire to possess; but essentially, when it is really love and not passion in isolation, it means the desire for union, for a complete sharing of life, rather than merely possession: it means the desire to live in love, to be possessed by love.

The soul is first of all feminine to reality. For Boethius, philosophy is (what the word itself means) the love of wisdom; but wisdom for him is a reality, that 'living thought which is the cause of all, and which is self-subsistent, God,' and which, illuminating the mind of man, draws him to itself by love. So it is that, in the *Consolation*, Philosophy comes to him as a woman, and leads him to Wisdom which also, in so many languages (*sophia, sapientia, sagesse*) is feminine.

And again, if we think at all in these days of the ideal of holiness it is probably in terms of heroic action, of those whom the love of God has driven to overcome great obstacles and achieve great things in the world; yet essentially, though of course activity of one kind or another follows—and often it is indeed a question of immense and all but incessant external activity in the world—

32

essentially, holiness consists not in doing but in being: St Paul's 'I live yet not I, but Christ liveth in me'; St Catherine of Genoa's 'My Me is God, nor do I know my selfhood save in him'; the Sanskrit formula, *Tat tvam asi*: 'That art thou'; the 'In truth who knows God becomes God' of the Mundaka Upanishad; the 'I exist in God and am altogether his' of the Mohammedan Rabi'a.

But no, the virus of the doctrine of 'justification by works' has eaten deep into the modern soul, when it thinks in terms of justification at all; even though the appalling figure of the *dévote* who is for ever busy *dans les oeuvres* but whose heart is black with envy and jealousy, hatred and spite, is there to mock us. Indeed, we are perhaps less likely to think of holiness (in any practical context) than of the 'formation of character': there, we feel, we are on solid ground; that is something we can put our hands to, something to grip on to; and perhaps, heaven help us, it is this that we teach our children. What a travesty, and a tragedy, to paint christianity simply in terms of character-building—the stiff upper lip, the straight bat, the categorical imperative! It is a travesty because it is likely to end in the smugness of self-made morality, in the arrogant self-reliance, self-complacency and scorn of the sinner which it is precisely the purpose of religion to destroy. It is a tragedy because at best, if this is what we teach the young, we give them the prose of christianity without the poetry, the dry bones instead of the living flesh and blood—and how then shall we expect them to be set on fire?

Holiness is the fruit of love and wisdom; and the first essential step to these is the sense of wonder: how shall we recapture it?

Benedictine monasticism, to which more than to any other single influence Europe owes its education, has as its motto the word *pax*: peace, tranquillity, quietude; and throughout the history of monasticism and of religious life in general one of the main elements in the training to wisdom and holiness has been *silentium*. To be aware you must first of all be still in soul; and physical silence is one of the great helps to the achieving of that stillness. Why do we suffer the appalling din in the midst of which we have to live? The ingenuity of man which devised the machines that make the noise could devise other machines to stop the noise.

(It has provided revolvers with silencers in the cause of successful murder; might it not provide other silencers in the cause of sanity?)

Why, again, do we suffer the appalling din of a speech which has become a 'purely animal, excretory function'? The incessant blare of the radio is doubled by the incessant clatter of what M. Picard calls 'verbal noise.' *Heureux deux amis*, said Péguy, *qui s'aiment assez pour (savoir) se taire ensemble.* When people who have no love for one another come together they talk feverishly all the time: they are afraid of what silence might reveal. Perhaps the same is true of certain verbose approaches to God. But there is no *pax* without *silentium*; and no wisdom without *pax*. St Peter Damian speaks of 'sheathing the sword of the tongue in the scabbard of silence'—*gladius linguae meae in taciturnitatis theca repositus*—and verbal din is indeed destructive; St Bede the Venerable mentions verbosity among the effects of accidie or sloth, that deep-seated boredom with divine things which poisons so profoundly the life of the spirit and in which no doubt we are to see one of the main causes of the restlessness, verbal and otherwise, of modern life.

But physical silence of itself will not produce inner stillness of soul; nor is that stillness absolutely dependent upon the existence of physical silence. If we cannot have silence, we must learn to do without it: to be still in soul despite the sound and the fury. We must learn to shut out the chaos; and to look and be aware and wonder and grow wise, in an enclave of inner silence in our own souls which no external din can destroy. The angel's announcement to Mary of her destiny was made to her in the stillness of her chamber, *sola sine comite, sola sine teste*: 'neither companion nor witness there,' as St Ambrose says, 'that what passed might not be debased in gossip'; but had it been made to her in the middle of the market-place she would not have been less attentive, or more conscious of her surroundings. (So the *Ancren Riwle* tells us: 'Sit ye with Mary stone-still at God's feet, and listen to him alone.')

The condition of awareness, of Finite and Infinite alike, is, in the words of Evelyn Underhill already quoted, 'a self-forgetting attentiveness, a profound concentration, a self-merging, which operates a real communion between the seer and the seen'; and she goes on to describe in practical detail what we are to do. ' All that is asked of us is that we shall look for a little time, in a special and undivided manner, at some simple, concrete, and external thing. This object of our contemplation may be almost anything we please: a picture, a statue, a tree, a distant hillside, a growing plant, running water, little living things. We need not, with Kant, go to the starry heavens. " A little thing the quantity of an hazel nut " will do for us, as it did for Lady Julian long ago.' (Indeed, it seems likely to be more helpful to take some tiny thing which one can hold in the palm of the hand—a leaf, a blade of grass, a pebble —and so the more easily concentrate upon it.) ' Remember, it is a practical experiment on which we are set; not an opportunity of pretty and pantheistic meditation.

' Look, then, at this thing which you have chosen. Wilfully yet tranquilly refuse the messages which countless other aspects of the world are sending; and so concentrate your whole attention on this one act of loving sight that all other objects are excluded from the conscious field. Do not think, but as it were pour out your personality towards it: let your soul be in your eyes. Almost at once, this new method of perception will reveal unsuspected qualities in the external world. First, you will perceive about you a strange and deepening quietness; a slowing down of our feverish mental time. Next, you will become aware of a heightened sig- nificance, an intensified existence in the thing at which you look. As you, with all your consciousness, lean out towards it, an answer- ing current will meet yours. It seems as though the barrier between its life and yours, between subject and object, had melted away. You are merged with it, in an act of true communion: and you *know* the secret of its being deeply and unforgettably, yet in a way which you can never hope to express. . . . The " eye which looks upon Eternity " has been given its opportunity. We have been immersed for a moment in the " life of the All ": a deep and peaceful love unites us with the substance of all things, a " Mystic Marriage " has taken place between the mind and some aspect of the external world. *Cor ad cor loquitur.*'[1]

[1] *op. cit.* pp. 301-2.

The author of course hastens to add that all this is in no sense 'to be equated with the transcendental contemplation of the mystic.' In prayer—this inward prayer, the silent awareness of and communion with the indwelling Spirit—the messages of the senses are to be excluded: it is the invisible God only whom the mind and heart must seek. But at least in the former case you are training yourself to know reality and not just to know about reality; and to that extent you are preparing the ground. You are also doing something of immense practical importance for the business of everyday living: you are learning to see and love things as ends and not just as means; and you are learning how to be rooted again in the universe.

You are also in touch once again with mystery; and so the mind and the heart can expand. Just as lovers in their moments of ecstasy (*ek-stasis*), of totally absorbed communion, whether inclusive of the height of physical passion or not, are caught up through their heightened consciousness into some sort of experience of transcendence, some breaking down of the normal barriers of individual life; so also, to learn through the senses (but, as with the æsthetic experience, to learn through the spirit living *in* the senses) the look and feel and smell of wood and stone, of leaf and pebble, of the fragile and funny furriness of a kitten, is to be liberated into a greater world, a world of mystery, and to know communion with it.

'Behind every landscape,' wrote Alain Fournier, 'I feel the landscape of my paradise.' It is what ought to be, universally; it is St Paul's 'from the foundations of the world men have caught sight of his invisible nature, his eternal power and his divineness, as they are known through his creatures.'[1] And let us note in passing that we have made this perception of mystery the harder for ourselves inasmuch as our soulless utilitarianism colours our attitude not only to things but to words as well. If we suffer—if not gladly at any rate with resignation and even a certain equanimity—the hideous jargon of the bureaucrat, instead of (like the king in the parable) sending out our soldiers to destroy those murderers of language and burn their cities, it must be because here again we

---

[1] *Romans*, I, 20.

have lost our sense of wonder and our reverence. For primitive peoples, words are endued with magic power; we, in our enlightened stupidity, neglect the power because we reject the magic.

Language used as it is meant to be used has beauty; it also has power. When Keats throws open his magic casements he makes real to us the faery lands forlorn; when Hopkins gives glory to God for dappled things he makes us see the things anew and live in the glory. So it is also with music; which can indeed make us feel bellicose or lustful or inspire in us feelings of earthiness or a deadly *ennui*, but on the other hand can lead us to the mountain-tops, can speak to us of other worlds, can show us the pain of man and the pity of God.

Words and music, sights and sounds, can then, if we look and listen with more than the outward eye and ear, reveal to us something of the mystery of being; and in so doing can lead us on much further: can give us some distant inkling of the infinite horizons which lie beyond. And to achieve something of that vision of and oneness with the Infinite is, primarily, to give to God the glory and the love which are his due, and to one's own life the depth and fullness and meaning which are his will for it; it is also to be able to give to humanity that help which each should be able to ask of all; it is also to give to these creature-things, the *visibilia* which have helped to lead one to the Invisible, their own chief glory as instruments of God in the making of man.

Those who achieve this wisdom, this union with the universe and the Love who makes the universe, are then in a position not only to enjoy all things but to use all things without danger of degradation. Other forms of knowledge will be theirs to use, because they will use them not arrogantly or narrowly but within the framework of their wisdom. Science will be theirs to use and apply, because the cosmos they study, the power they wield, is for them the 'earth and its fullness' which is the Lord's, and the greatest glory of which is to give glory to the Lord. All things will be theirs to use, because they will use them not merely as means but as having value in themselves, and so they will approach them with wonder and reverence. They can concern themselves with immediate causes without disaster, because beyond the immediate they will always sense the ultimate. They can and will give themselves to activity, and the activity will be beneficent, because behind the action will be the vision, behind the power will be the love, behind the energy will be the understanding and the humility.

'Launch out into the deep.' It is difficult to do, in the midst of the noise and the chaos, the bustle, the frenzy, where an endless multiplicity of things engages the surface of the mind. But even physical silence is something which it is possible to achieve: you can shut out, at least at times, the sound and the fury and be at peace; and inner stillness of soul is something which can be achieved and which, being achieved, can continue no matter what the external conditions.

Then you can launch out into the deep: that inner deep which is the 'fund of the spirit,' the fine point of the soul where infinity is to be found, the infinity of the indwelling Spirit. Then you can launch out into the deep because you can learn, in the words of the *De Adhaerendo Deo*, to 'accept everything that happens to you, whatever its cause, in silence, in stillness and with an even mind, as coming to you from the Father's hand and from his divine providence.' Then you can launch out into the deep because you can imitate the man of whom the same book speaks, who 'withdraws wholly into himself' and 'when he has shut out and forgotten all creatures he dwells with Christ in stillness; . . . and summoning up the whole bent and power of his love, he pours himself into God with all the strength of his inmost soul.' Then you can launch out into the deep because you can understand something of what Henry Suso meant when he wrote: 'Be steadfast, and never rest content until thou hast obtained the now of eternity as thy present possession in this life, so far as this is possible to human infirmity;' you can launch out into the deep because you can understand the words of Hindu wisdom: 'What lies beyond life shines not to the childish, careless, deluded by wealth. "This is the only world: there is no other," they say; and they go to death again and again;' and you can understand equally those other words from the same source: 'Who sees all beings

38

in his own Self, and his own Self in all beings, loses all fear; ' for ' in God there is no fear.'

But to launch out into the deep is to make our whole attitude to life, to law, to conduct, to truth, more and more inward. We have already considered the difference between mere character, expressing itself in outward irreproachability of conduct, and holiness, expressing itself essentially in a state of being. We shall have occasion later on to contrast similarly two notions of law, as an external restraint or as an expression of love inscribed in the heart. We have thought too of the return of mind to its funda-mental purposes: to wonder, adoration, vision, wisdom, all of which can spring only from inward humility and receptivity. And within the Church, too, there would seem to be a similar duty incumbent upon christians: precisely to ' internalize ' the lessons which the Church is all the time trying to teach us. Guardini has warned us against the danger which arises ' from the discipline that produces external order, dragoons life into a fixed mould, and, itself inspired by fear and uncertainty, represses all independent movement.' ' Our moral life,' he writes, ' is becoming impoverished because it is becoming a mere matter of routine: because for long, under the influence of a rationalist ethical code, of Kantian for-malism, and of an empty moral schematism, it was regarded as a fulfilment of prescriptions. It is not, however. We have but to listen to Plato to feel, here, in the first conscious exposition of the problem, the whole creative quality of ethical action. Moral action is concerned, therefore, with making humanly real that which is not yet thus real: with giving an earthly form to the Eternal and Infinite.'[1] And what, in the last resort, gives earthly form to the Infinite is love; for God is love.

We have to thank some modern catholic novelists, among others, for greatly increasing our understanding of what might be called the theology of weakness.[2] Mr. Graham Greene's *The Power and the Glory*, for instance, portrays a bad priest, a priest whose life is

---

[1] Guardini: *Conscience*, pp. 12, 32.

[2] I have tried to deal with certain aspects of this in the introductory chapter to *The Seven Swords: The Sinner Who Looks like a Saint*.

In the four paragraphs which follow here, I again make use of material from *The Problem of the Catholic Novelist* previously referred to.

very far indeed from being a 'fulfilment of prescriptions' which ought in fact to have governed it, but who none the less ends by accepting martyrdom for being a priest. Is he then a saint as well as a sinner? Can holiness be compatible with weakness? M. Mauriac wrote a preface to the French edition of the book in which he described how, 'as he approaches his end, we see this mediocre sinner slowly conforming himself to Christ till he comes to resemble him—or rather, for this is not strong enough—to identify himself with his Lord and God.' This statement provoked strong criticism. It was a blasphemy, one critic wrote, to identify with Christ and the saints this sinner who got drunk on the eve of his death and who had previously found it impossible to resist this and other vices. And the same critic went on to accuse the author of lutheranism, for contrasting sin not with virtue but with faith. There is surely here a double confusion.

In the first place, to be identified with means to be united with, not to be equal in all respects to. The priest is very far indeed from giving perfect ' earthly form to the Infinite.' But while he cannot, and knows that he cannot, reach up to God to be united with him, God can reach down, and does reach down, to unite himself with the humble of heart, despite their sins and their squalors. How little we understand the Passion of Christ unless we understand at least that! Perhaps the deepest mystery of redemption and divine love is precisely that we can be redeemed not merely *from* our squalors but, in a sense, *in* our squalors. If holiness did mean possessing God we might well despair; but holiness means being possessed by God, and so in spite of our frailties and betrayals we can continue to hope: the Word is long since descended into us: there is nothing there that can frighten him now. Russian spirituality, which has so deep an insight into the meaning of the ' humiliated Christ,' gives us the unforgettable story of the old missionary who, when rebuked by his bishop for speaking too familiarly of Christ, replied: ' He does not mind simplicity. Who can tell his generation—yet he walked with the shepherds, he went with the sinners, he did not abhor the mangy sheep. Whenever he found one he put it as it was on his holy shoulders and carried it to his Father. Now, what could the Father do? He did not want to grieve his

40

Son the sufferer—so for his sake he let the untidy thing into his sheepfold.'

There is a second confusion in the criticism of Mauriac's words which we were considering. The contrast in *The Power and the Glory* is not, surely, between sin and faith; it is between sin (of a certain kind) and love of God: between weakness and *caritas*. What the story suggests to us is that a man can in fact love God enough to sacrifice his life for him even while remaining incapable through weakness of avoiding this or that sin; for if the priest does give his life in the end, even though it be in this undignified, rather desperate, rather passive sort of way, it proves not faith merely but love; and if he has to get drunk in order to go through with it, still it leaves the essential fact unchanged.

Once again, therefore, holiness (or some not too distant approach to holiness) is a question of love, of the *will* to serve, even though the love is normally far from perfect and the will is weak. True, there is a danger here of serious misunderstanding: we should miss the point of the lesson completely if we were tempted by it to a *pecca fortiter*: to a complacent persuasion that we have no need to worry about our own sins, or even that we do well to sin in order the better to plumb the depths of God's mercy—forgetting that weakness is compatible with growth in love only when the weakness, the evil, is hated and strenuously resisted. We may need also to be reminded of the danger of a *pharisaisme du publicain*: a sort of pride in being a sinner because at least thereby one is not as the Pharisee. We need the help of the theologian to make precisions which we must not expect from the novelist working in his own medium; and theology will explain first, how heredity, environment, physical or psychological states, difficulties of temperament and so on can lessen (or indeed destroy) the voluntariness and therefore the guilt of human actions; secondly, how an evil habit, sincerely repented but not yet eradicated, lessens the guilt of any subsequent act proceeding from the habit; how therefore holiness is indeed compatible with continuing frailties, and how God in his mercy and through the workings of his divine life in the soul can in the end bring forth out of this mixture of good and evil an act of love which is heroic—far greater in its intensity than was the normal habitual love existing hitherto in the soul.

And as we need to internalize our idea of holiness, so too with the other lessons the Church teaches us. It is perhaps not without significance in this context that we tend so much nowadays to speak of religious realities in the plural instead of the singular: the plural which denotes the externalized effect or expression rather than the singular which expresses the inward cause, the state of being. We tend to speak, and think, of sins instead of sinfulness; of graces instead of indwelling divine life and power; of affections instead of love, of prayers instead of prayer, of acts of contrition instead of sorrow.

Again, are we perhaps too content to rest in formulas instead of struggling to some measure of deep awareness of the reality that lies behind the formulas? The formulas are of course essential: they express for us, in terms with which the human mind can grapple, truths about the Infinite which we need, absolutely, to know. But the propositions themselves are not the Reality; and the Church has other ways of leading us to that Reality which would themselves 'internalize' the propositions and bring us closer to the Ineffable.[1] We learn by listening to and assimilating the Church's dogmatic teaching; but we learn also by living the Church's life, living the Church's symbols, letting the life sink into us and form us, letting our whole personalities be moulded by the wood and the fire and the water.

But the christian cannot be content to find life himself in vision and inwardness while ignoring the plight of his fellow-men. If he must fight against the externalization of his own life, he must fight also against the externalization of life in the world at large. He must fight against the growing tide of utilitarianism in education; against the idea of work as merely a wage-earning but subhuman drudgery; against the sort of law-making which leads to regimentation and the destruction of personal values; against systems which have no place for leisure as creative contemplation; against the use of mind as simply a means to possession and power.

He must pray and labour and struggle for a renewal of wisdom,

---

[1] Cf. *infra*, chs. IV-VI.

for a recapturing of the sense of wonder and reverence, for a return to a contemplative spirit, for a re-birth of philosophy as the love of that Wisdom which ' is the cause of all ' and which draws men to itself by love; and he must hope that he and his fellow christians, having learnt more deeply and more fully the inward meaning of things, may indeed in the end be able to give ' an earthly form to the Eternal' and so become instruments of the Spirit in his work of leading mankind to that fullness of life for which it was created.

III

Education: The Search for Wisdom

CASSIODORUS, long ago, wrote of the ' vast leisure of the cloister ': it was that leisure that educated Europe. As we have seen, without leisure—in the sense not of an idle vacuity of mind, but of the deep stillness of contemplation—culture is impossible; and it is a measure of the task which confronts education today that not only the reality but even the idea of leisure in any such sense is so largely lost to our world. And it would seem, unfortunately, that powerful trends in the educational world, so far from attempting to remedy the destructive tendencies in modern life which we have been considering, are on the contrary co-operating uncritically and whole-heartedly with them.

We have been thinking of the frenzied tempo, the confusion, the activism, of modern life, its hatred or fear of silence and stillness. Education could set itself to combat this state of affairs; but in fact it is itself too often determined by the prevailing atmosphere; and becomes itself a frenzied rush, a scramble for examination marks, for degrees and diplomas; it becomes itself so activist that there is no time to think and live; it becomes itself so utilitarian that it defeats its own essential ends; it may provide a great deal of information, it can hardly hope to be a royal road to a deep and vivid culture. The *litterae humaniores* seem indeed to be fighting a somewhat despondent rearguard action; and when a society loses the humanities it must inevitably in the end lose its humanity. It is indeed ' important that through the ancient languages that are " useless," man should be redeemed from the world of mere profit

44

and utility. We cannot " do much " with the ancient languages, but they bring us into touch with something that takes us beyond the world of pure expedience.'[1]

We have been thinking of the degree to which modern man has lost his roots in Nature, of how the rhythm of life, the budding and growing of plant and tree, the cycle of the seasons, have become for him a closed book, so that he cannot learn, as the poets and mystics learn, to make all this life their own, to become one with the universe. And again education could do much to remedy the state of affairs; but it will not do so if all the time it is concerned simply with utilities and if its own setting—the vast barrack-like urban school—and its own atmosphere—of chilly intellectual utilitarianism—are as unnatural as anything else in the modern city.

We have been thinking of man's loss of his natural human setting, the loss of the home, and of how the lack of a creative home life just as surely produces rootlessness as the broken homes of divorced and re-married parents produce psychological maladjustments in their children. Again education might do something to redeem the situation; but it certainly will not do so if it is itself not homely in atmosphere but impersonal, not concerned with leading the young towards humanity, creativeness, wisdom, but

[1] M. Picard, *op. cit.* p. 60. Some interesting sidelights on the loss of the whole idea of the ' utility of the useless ' to which we referred in the first chapter are to be found in the sphere of ' play,' which, as Mr Donald Nichol points out in an article on the subject (*Blackfriars*, March 1952), is not only closely correlated by St Thomas with contemplation, but also provides the ' best analogy by which most of us can reach towards some conception of God's creative act '—in creating the world out of nothing. But ' we of the twentieth century have abandoned the creaturely receptive attitude of contemplation or play and replaced it by the ideal of the captain of commerce who wrests time and nature to his purpose. When he says that " time is money " the modern business-man is quoting a formula for the destruction of himself and our culture.' And ' having for centuries asked what *use* everything is, he has eventually turned his eyes towards our play. When we tell him that we do not need to state a *use* for our play, because it is delightful in itself, he is incapable of understanding us. He has so thoroughly perverted his own nature that he is incapable of *enjoying* anything, including our delightful play. And so, in his jaundiced perversity, he has even turned what was our play into an article of commerce, by inventing professional sport, and making it an occasion for gambling. Having lost the capacity for play he has poisoned the play of others. But this captain of commerce will not have the last word. For if you wander into cities which his bombs and shells have reduced to rubble, you will still find " the city full of boys and girls, playing in the streets thereof." They laugh as they play over the business-man's destruction; these children prove themselves true men—in St Thomas's definition of man—a " rational animal capable of laughter." And in the last day they shall laugh, these children in the rubble, when they walk the streets of the New Jerusalem, playing before the face of God.'

simply with turning them into successful examinees and efficient technicians or 'functionaries.'

What then is the most important function of education today? Before attempting to answer the question in any definitive way, let us go back for a moment to the simple first principles of the thing.

A human being is a psycho-physical unity, with certain aptitudes or potentialities in the development and creative use of which he will find his happiness and fulfilment. These potentialities are partly individual, as one man has it in him to be a good baker and another to be a good candlestick-maker; and partly general, as all men are made up of body, mind and heart which can be developed in one way or another into a full, rich, deep, harmonious and creative personality, giving glory to God and happiness and peace to men. Of these two kinds of potentialities the general are in the last resort of far greater importance than the individual, though a technological society will no doubt of its very nature tend to adopt and inculcate the opposite view. It is far more important to be a great personality than to be a great butcher or baker: one proof of which is that you can achieve great success in the business of life, amass a great fortune or acquire great power and prestige and eminence, and yet know in your heart that you have failed, you have not followed your star. The same is true when you think in terms of the 'common good': the 'great figures' of history benefit humanity only in so far as they are in fact great personalities; apart from that we are indebted not to the tycoons, the captains of industry, the demagogues, the conquerors,[1] but to the starveling poets, the derided geniuses, the quiet lovers of wisdom, the humble saints and the hidden mystics; we look, above all, away from the 'wisdom of this world' to the folly of the Cross.

What then is a great personality? Because man is a many-levelled creature, his growth must include the development of the various levels; but it must be a development in harmony, in unity. Thus the development of the body is important not as an end in itself but as part of the development of the whole personality to fullness of life; the senses need to be developed and trained but

---

[1] 'Greatness,' wrote Fielding in *Jonathan Wild*, ' consists in bringing all manner of mischief on mankind, and Goodness in removing it from them.'

again not to an independent life but to the whole personality's awareness of and connaturality with the true, the good and the beautiful. The same is true of the emotional level; which if wisely trained can serve the spirit by adding its powerful drive to the search for truth and goodness, but which otherwise can either come to dominate the personality to the eclipse of mind, or on the other hand can lead, through suppression and atrophy, to a desiccation and frustration which will warp the whole personality. At the same time, though the aim is to integrate all these levels into a unity, they must of course be each addressed directly: must have truth and goodness and beauty presented to them each in their own way. Hence the importance, for example, of the material setting of a school: the buildings themselves beautiful, dignified, and at the same time having the atmosphere of home, not of an impersonal institution; the setting, if not the countryside at least something akin to it; the curriculum concerned not merely with absorbing information but with creative activity—in paint, in wood, in words, in agriculture and so on; the relationship between teachers and pupils easy, personal, uninhibited, homely.

Where the education of the mind is concerned there is again a scale of values. It is more important to know and love the *B Minor Mass* than to know the date of it; more important to know the sea, and all the wealth of its symbolism, than to know the names of the national seaports; more important to know the look and feel of good wood, glass, silver, than to know its date or its cost. Information there must be; criticism, discrimination there must be; but beneath the rational development there is the intuitive life, which is so often maimed by rationalism or utilitarianism, by the ' shades of the prison house '; and because today the emphasis has so long been placed—and latterly has been placed to so extreme a degree—on the rational, the scientific, there is urgent need of a readjustment of balance, or rather of discovering a *modus docendi* which shall address itself to the mind as a whole. (Thus science should always be taught, in these days especially, by a humanist, whose scientific equipment has not dimmed his vision, his sense of the *lacrimae rerum*, his love of the ' secret heart of things,' his intuition that the ' earth is the Lord's and the fullness thereof.')

For in these days we have to struggle consciously to learn what other ages learnt unconsciously: the deep lessons of Nature and of humanity's great universal symbols. We have to re-learn the lesson that the first thing is to receive and accept: to lay open the mind and heart to reality and let it flood in and take possession. It is good to know what science has to tell us of the sun, but not if the knowledge destroys for us the 'great purring lion,' the sun-god who goes down at night into the sea to be re-born next day at dawn; it is good to know what biology and geology and botany and the rest can teach us, but only if at the same time we know what it is to lie with face buried in the grass, learning the earth; to lie with a hand in the rippling waters of a stream, learning the water; to hold in the hollow of our hands the leaf, the acorn, the pebble, listening to the essences of things; to know the feel and texture of the flower's petal, the fur of an animal, and to know in them all the Presence which is all about them.

Education, in other words, has as one of its primary objects to teach us how to stop and be still and look, how to concentrate our gaze till things begin to reveal their mystery to us. It must teach us to preserve and heighten our sense of wonder, which is the womb of poetry and of philosophy alike; for otherwise, no matter what our book-learning, beauty and life will pass us by.

It is the same when we come to think of the training of heart and will: we can express it in terms of virtue, of character; but if we do we shall express a half-truth. The aim is to produce free, responsible, creative personalities, loving God and goodness and acting in accord with what they love. But that is more than character; it is not the chilly rectitude of duty for duty's sake. It is not prose only but poetry; not character only but (in the end) holiness; not only the virtues but the 'wind that bloweth where it listeth,' the breath of the Spirit, the fresh, spontaneous, lyrical quality you find in its fullness in the saints. Here, somehow, must be discovered the principles of a sound pedagogy of discipline: we cannot hope to achieve these results by regimentation, forcing, rigid sanctions, still less by the routine learning of a catechism by heart. The Church gives us a perfect example of a wise, balanced, formation by simultaneously instructing our minds through dogma and our hearts through symbols, through the things, words, actions, gestures which make up its liturgical life.[1] For the object of these latter, in terms of their human effects, is to form personalities of such a kind that they will in fact in the end fall in love with what is supremely lovable and so will want their lives to conform to it. But the lesson, the deep unconscious lesson, will be lost unless at the conscious level there is freedom: uninhibited freedom to discuss any and every theological problem and difficulty, freedom about attendance at church services, freedom in the sense that religious instruction is as far removed as possible from the atmosphere of competitive examinations and sanctions. How can we ever forgive ourselves if we reduce the Beauty ever old and ever new to the level of a chemistry examination paper?

Now it is true that religious education is not to be regarded as just a part, even the most important part, of education in general: it is the whole of education, in the sense that everything that is taught should lead back, directly or indirectly, to God, and should help to inculcate a point of view which in fact is the religious point of view. If the sciences are being studied, they are concerned with the earth which is the Lord's; if the arts, they reveal beauties which are a remote reflection of Beauty; if history is in question, it must always in the end be brought back to the central moment in human history which is the re-creative death of the Word. To teach a loving awareness of Nature must be to teach also that the *lacrimae rerum*, the tragedy of a beauty which is fleeting, is not the last word; to encourage the development of a whole and integrated personality is to help the vision to open on to infinite horizons, the heart to be conscious of its infinite potentialities, desires and needs.

So that in the end all education is seen as an education in the knowledge and love and service of God: the care and training of the body as a care for the temple of God, the training of the senses as a concern for the beauty which reflects ultimate Beauty and is redolent of its presence, the quest for knowledge and wisdom as formed ultimately by a sense of ultimate values, and all forms of wisdom as part of that divine wisdom which is the gift of the

[1] Cf. *infra*, ch. VI.

Spirit, all intuitive life as part of the life of prayer, of the inchoate vision of God.

And as the purpose of education is to produce creative personalities—makers in art, in love, in home, in society—so especially is it to produce personalities who will share with the redemptive Word in his work of re-creating the world, and who will do so precisely through all these other forms of making: turning their lives, their work, their homes, through *caritas* into the worship of God and the redeeming of man.

In other words, the humanism which is the aim of christian education is all the time a christian humanism, a ' humanism of the Cross': which means, not the pursuit of a pagan, a profane culture in one department with religious belief and practice in another, but a culture impregnated, in-formed through and through with the love of God and an understanding of the purposes and the pity of God. It means that culture is seen all the time within the framework of a world sin-laden but redeemed: in terms of that pattern of descent and re-ascent, that dark journey through death to life, from egocentricity to love, which as we shall see is the whole burden of the christian fulfilment of the ancient myths. It means the very opposite of that ivory-tower æstheticism which averts its gaze from the squalors of humanity: it means the love of all beauty, but also a humble and loving descent into the depths, the squalors and the ugliness, in order to find God there; it means seeing the beauty *against* that background of sin and redemption, and therefore with deep sorrow and pity. It means the love of beauty lived in poverty of spirit; it means judgment and criticism in humility of heart; it means initiative, responsibility, creativeness, springing from gentleness and the sense of sin; it means maturity of mind in terms of adoring friendship with the redeeming Word; in fine, it means that all life, all love, all knowledge are part of that *caritas* which alone gives wisdom to human love and experience.

A bad educational system can do untold harm to the child, the boy or girl, the man or woman. It can take the pupil with all his potentialities for greatness and kill the vision within him. It can warp him; it can make him a half-man or a sub-man; it can stuff him with knowledge and leave him foolish; it can paint over him a veneer of piety and leave him unliberated; it can take away his birthright for a mess of pottage. But where it is trying its best to lead human beings to fullness of life in God, then there is no measuring the good it can do—and it may indeed be one of the main hopes for the survival of our civilization. For then it will be teaching human beings to be still and wonder, and above all to wonder at and to live with God; it will be teaching them to become whole personalities, above all through becoming identified with Christ; it will be teaching them to love and live with Nature, above all as reflecting and revealing God; to love and live with other human beings, above all as part of the all-embracing love of God; to understand what home is through being itself homely, what personalism is through being itself personal, what the love of God is through being itself God-filled; it will be teaching them to understand and to live every dark journey as part of that one supreme journey which leads indeed to fullness of life because to that life which is eternal, that home which is eternal, the fulfilment of all desires and needs and potentialities together: the *interminabilis vitae tota simul et perfecta possessio*, which is the endless praise and glory of God, the joy and happiness of all the saints.

All education then is in the end to be an education to wisdom, an education to God. But when we consider religious instruction as such, in the technical sense: how can it best be done? Let us think here, not merely of education in the early days at school, but of education in the widest sense: the education which begins indeed in school and university but must go on throughout life— for if we ever stop educating ourselves we resign ourselves to mental stagnation and death.

If Léon Bloy was right when he said that there is only one sorrow, that of not being a saint, we may presumably go back a stage and say that there is only one problem, that of coming to know God. And first of all, can we really have certain knowledge *that* he is, and, to some extent at least, certain knowledge of *what* he is? The climate of opinion in which we live is such as to make us feel that the possibility of real certitude is a remote one: that if God is not a long-since exploded fantasy, he is at best a more or less plausible hypothesis. And the influence of a prevailing climate of opinion is very great; and may lead, even in the mind of the professing christian, to a weakening of faith, to a split in his personality between the realities to which he gives formal allegiance in religious profession and the realities on which in fact he bases his everyday life and conduct.

Again, the christian faith is to be a *credo ut intelligam*: a faith which looks towards understanding and is itself a *rationabile obsequium*, a service which is not only not incompatible with reason but is in large measure vouched for by reason. But the modern world has little trust in speculative reason, in philosophy: we are all too familiar with the view that metaphysics is mere moonshine; and even when a speculative line of argument seems to be incontrovertibly valid and no logical flaw can be found in it, nothing is easier for modern man than to stop short at a sort of purely formal acknowledgement of its correctitude without allowing the conclusion reached to exercise any influence on conduct or on any deep level of the mind.

It seems in consequence important to emphasize the fact that there are more ways than one of coming to the knowledge of God; and that the different ways are complementary; and that nowadays especially we need them all.

Christians continue to hold, in their bluff, homespun, backwoods sort of way, that the mind can attain to knowledge—and to certain knowledge: not just a persuasion, even a firm persuasion, but complete certitude—of the fact of God's existence: of the existence, that is, of a supreme Being, Pure Actuality, Unmoved Mover; and can predicate, also with certitude, certain attributes of that Being: unity, simplicity, infinity, perfection, immateriality. It can proceed, by the *via remotionis*, to say that this supreme Being is Spirit (mind-will), is Truth, is Goodness, is Beauty, is Love. Incidentally, it will not be dismayed by facile talk, in Freudian vein, of projections and Father-figures, or of crude anthropomorphisms. For the latter, while it is true that the *via remotionis* proceeds by stripping of their imperfections, their limitations, the relevant qualities which we find in our human experience, and so of attributing them to God, it is essentially not a question of taking human qualities and applying them with modifications to God, but of taking divine qualities and applying them with modifications to creatures; for men, as St Thomas puts it, are good, for example, only as having some share in goodness: it is God alone who is goodness itself; and when we say that God is Love we are not taking some definition of our human love and saying that God must be like that: we are discovering as best we can what love in itself is like and then acknowledging that that is what our human love is meant remotely to resemble. So far from trying to attribute human characteristics to God, the christian is supposed all the time to be trying to realize some sort of shadowy reflection of divine characteristics in himself. As for the Freudian attitude to religion in general and to God the Father in particular, which still largely ' doth infect the air,' subsequent developments in the field of psychology itself have radically altered the picture. As Fr Victor White puts it in his important study, *God and the Unconscious*, ' Freud, in effect, is turned upside down by Jung, in much the same way as Hegel had been turned upside down by Marx. Freud's data are accepted and indeed amplified; but their significance is inverted ': behind the physical father there is the archetypal Father, but the latter appears now ' not as a phantasy-substitute for the first; but rather does the first appear as a particular manifestation and symbol of the second. The way is now open to us . . . no longer to conceive of God as a substitute for the physical father, but rather the physical father as the infant's first substitute for God. . . . God is less a Big Father than the physical father a little god. Clearly we are not far from St Paul's " Father . . . from whom all father-hood (*patria*) in heaven and in earth is named ".'[1]

But to return to the ' way of reason ' in general: it is not an easy way, for it is not easy to philosophize; and if it is the only way available—as often for modern man it is, because of all that he has lost of other aspects of his human heritage—it puts upon the plain man, as Mr C. S. Lewis has pointed out, a burden which the plain man ought not to be asked to bear. And even if in fact a man

[1]White: *God and the Unconscious*, pp. 55-57.

is equipped to undertake it, still he will have to reckon, as we have seen, with the prevailing climate of opinion, the prevailing scepticism and agnosticism where reason is concerned; and so it is of vital importance to re-capture the second way—and an essential task of education to impart the knowledge of it. It is the way of symbolism.

With the birth of the modern world, as Guardini notes, ' man lost his living contact with real things: he became the man of the towns, of ideologies, of formulas. The whole of existence became artificial. The profound order of life was turned upside down. The natural rhythms of day and night, of the seasons, were no longer felt. . . . Man could no longer perceive the message of things . . . he could only see them now in the light of brute matter, as objects of pursuit and possession, of commerce or research.'[1]

As we lose touch with real things, we lose the lessons which we could learn intuitively from them: we forget humanity's symbols. Down through the ages of history men have learnt something of the deeper secrets of life from symbols: from the myths and legends, the fairy-tales and folk-lore, from the great dramas and poems. But today, symbolism is all but lost to us; the poets use it, the painters use it, above all the Church uses it, but modern life and modern education can blind us to the riches that are there; the secular heritage, the wisdom of the ages, is still ours to claim, but the modern way of life ignores and neglects it. If we need dramatic proof of the abyss into which we have fallen, we need do no more than mingle with the crowd in some shopping centre and watch and listen, or spend an hour or two with the Light Programme on the wireless, and then re-read the famous and sublime passage in Traherne's *Centuries of Meditations*: ' The corn was orient and immortal wheat which never should be reaped nor was ever sown. I thought it had stood from everlasting to everlasting. The dust and stones of the city were as precious as gold: the gates were at first the end of the world. The green trees when I saw them first through one of the gates transported and ravished me; their sweetness and unusual beauty made my heart to leap, and almost mad with ecstasy, they were such strange

---

[1] Guardini: *L'Esprit de la Liturgie*, p. 66.

and wonderful things. . . . Boys and girls tumbling in the streets were moving jewels: I knew not that they were born or should die. But all things abided eternally as they were in their proper places. Eternity was manifest in the Light of the Day, and something infinite behind everything appeared, which talked with my expectation and moved my desire. The City seemed to stand in Eden or to be built in Heaven.'

We lose sight of the intimations of immortality because we are immersed in the light of common day; we will not stop and look and so allow things to lead us into communion with something vaster, something infinite in which all things are one; we will not stop and learn from the imagery of things, the great universal symbols, to understand the deep truths about our human nature and human destiny.

Down through the ages men have treasured and learnt from the myth of the dark journey, the water-symbolism: the hero-myth which appears again and again under an endless variety of forms but expresses always the one essential theme: the night-journey through the dark waters, the dark forests or caverns; the struggle with dragon or serpent or sorcerer; the death; the rebirth. And the myths themselves do but express in one way what the religious rites, the sacrifices of humanity express in another: for in these latter there is again the same pattern: the offering and death of the victim, the acceptance and apotheosis (the victim becoming in some manner endued with divine life), and so the coming of that same divine life to the offerers.

All these things express something which is universally found in human history because it is part of the very stuff of humanity as we know it: a yearning for life, for rebirth, for liberation into a greater mode of existence; and a yearning which recognizes that in some way or other the life must be sought in death, the light must be found in darkness, the ascent must follow and be made possible by a previous descent. 'Except the grain of wheat, falling into the ground, die, itself remaineth alone'; 'except a man be born of water and of the Spirit, he cannot enter into the kingdom.' The sun dies in the evening and goes down into the waters of the sea, to be born again when the night is over; the winter darkness succeeds the autumn, the 'fall,' and the year dies, to be born again in the spring; the victim is slain on the altar; the hero does battle and dies; and all these things express something which is true of humanity as a whole: that the only way to find life in its fullness is in some sense or other to lose it.

Now it might be argued that while these things are indeed 'psychologically true,' they take us no further than the obvious fact that the way to wholeness lies through self-discipline and training; that the myth of rebirth is no more than a poetic metaphor for the humdrum business of the formation of character. But even the briefest contemplation of the 'pattern' is enough to show that whatever else it may mean it certainly cannot just mean that. Not for nothing do the fairy-tales traditionally end with the statement that hero and heroine lived happily *ever* after. The intimations are intimations of immortality; and the death is a door which opens on to infinity. 'The roots of our thoughts and feelings,' wrote Dostoevsky, 'are not here but in other worlds,' and if the sense of oneness with those other worlds 'grows weak or is destroyed in you the heavenly growth will die in you. Then you will be indifferent to life or even grow to hate it.' So, for instance, Dr Pieper suggests that 'perhaps the reason why "purely academic" has sunk to mean something sterile, pointless and unreal is *because* the *schola* has lost its roots in religion and in divine worship'; or again points out that 'there is no such thing as a feast "without Gods" . . . no such thing as a feast that does not ultimately derive its life from divine worship, and that does not draw its vitality as a feast from divine worship'[1]: for without worship there is only the dreariness of a 'Bank Holiday' or the grim regimentation of a 'Labour Day.' Fulfilled or unfulfilled, the yearning is a yearning not for any purely human life or wholeness, but for a life which is divine, for the Whole.

But is it in fact unfulfilled? To say that the symbols point to God is not to say that God in fact exists; to say that the myths depict the way to wholeness is not to say that the way in fact lies open before us. Now it is true that for the christian the shadow has given place to the substance, the story has been realized in

[1] *op. cit.* pp. 71-2, 77.

history, the poetic pattern has become a matter of hard historical fact: the agony and sacrificial death, in a definite place and at a definite moment of recorded history, of Christ the son of Mary. Here, as we shall see[1] are to be found a number of features which recur over and over again in the old stories, a pattern is drawn which recalls the pattern common to the old sacrifices. But do not these similarities lead one to suppose that the 'christian myth' is no more 'real' than any of the other myths, and so undermine the christian's faith? The very opposite is the case.

First of all, because, as Fr White points out, the similarities, striking though they indeed are, are not so striking as the differences. The first difference is precisely the *matter-of-factness* of the christian story. 'However many features we may find in the accounts of the Passion and Resurrection which resemble those of ritual and mythology,' he writes, 'those features are embedded in matter-of-fact historical narrative about events that take place, not in the sanctuary or the theatre, but in the workaday world of fact;' the 'very incidents which may strike us as the most poetical and mythological, which display the closest resemblance to the archetypal ritual pattern, are inextricably interwoven by the evangelists with down-to-earth existence at its most personal and individual, its most prosaic and even squalid; and it is precisely in and through this that they see the transcendent mystery'; in other words, this is not history being mythologized but the precise opposite, it is myth being realized in history; and Fr White quotes the words of Georges Berguer: 'Jesus had incarnated in his death and resurrection an inner experience that had existed potentially for centuries in the human soul, but that had never passed beyond the sphere of the dream. He translated into life the secular dream of the peoples.'[2]

The dream becomes real life; which means in psychological terms that 'the unconscious projection is now withdrawn: it is now interiorized, made fully conscious, and is now voluntarily *lived* out—no longer blindly, instinctively, periodically just *acted*.'[3] So the hero's combat, his *agon*, becomes the wholly interior agony in the garden; the sacrifice becomes a willing self-sacrifice (the

---

[1] Cf. *infra*, ch. IV. [2] *op. cit.* pp. 226-7. [3] White, *op. cit.* pp. 227-8.

second essential difference) and (the third) it is not recurrent but final, once and for all—' " Christ, rising from the dead, dieth now *no more*. Death shall *no more* have dominion over him. For in that he died to sin, he died *once*; but in that he liveth, he liveth unto God." (*Rom.* vi, 9-10.) Just because it has been lived and died out in fact and history, consciously and voluntarily, the myth is not destroyed but fulfilled; its endless repetition is broken together with its unconscious, compulsive power. Indeed, in becoming fact it ceases to be mere myth.'[1]

St Thomas Aquinas holds that it is impossible for a *naturale desiderium*, a desire so fundamental as to be part of human nature itself, to be unrealizable.[2] What is so striking—and what, so far from undermining faith, brings it so massive a support—is that if you accept hypothetically the truth of the christian view of the existence and nature of God (' God is love ') and of the incarnation, it becomes evident at once that everything *coheres*: God creates man with this nature, these yearnings; but if he is love he cannot leave the nature and the yearnings (and, incidentally, the myths which express them) unfulfilled; and so the Word is made flesh and himself lives out the ' pattern ': his life and death fulfil the myth so that it ceases to be mere myth; his sacrifice fulfils all sacrifices and takes the place of all other sacrifices; and there is exact correspondence between the needs and desires of humanity, and the expression of the needs, and the fulfilment once and for all of the needs.

But the universality of the myth can be a support to faith in

[1] *ibid.* pp. 228-9. For the christian, of course, the full revelation of God's nature and love and pity, and of the supernatural character of man's redemption and ' new ' life, far transcends the aspirations expressed in the myth-pattern, leading as it does to the final glory of the ' things no eye has seen, no ear has heard, no human heart conceived, the welcome God has prepared for those who love him ' (I *Corinth.* ii, 9).

[2] This principle might well seem to provide an example of what was said above of the difficulty of finding conviction in the rational approach to God when the prevailing climate of opinion is antagonistic to the principles and presuppositions of such an approach. The principle here in question depends for its validity on the principle of finality, which itself derives from the principle of ' sufficient reason ': every thing, every nature, which exists must have some end-purpose (*omne agens agit propter finem*), for otherwise it would have no *raison d'être*—which would mean that the contingent (which does not exist of itself) would at the same time be unconditioned (i.e. would exist of itself), which is absurd. But this argument, which is basic in the aristotelean-thomist tradition, will not be likely to appeal to a world which acquiesces in the appeal of the unattainable, the ineluctability of the absurd and the ambiguous, the nostalgic beauty of the hopelessly unrealizable, of Laforgue's *Comme ils sont beaux, les trains manqués* . . .

another way. Fr White points out again how 'fifty years or so ago it seems to have been widely supposed that these discoveries of similarity between christian and pagan mysteries . . . somehow made nonsense of christianity. And it must be admitted that they did make nonsense of a great many nineteenth-century ideas *about* christianity: they made it impossible at least to regard it just as some sort of transcendental ethic, dropped ready-made from the sky, without roots in the earth, in history, without relevance to the basic and perennial needs of human society and the human psyche, or to the forms and forces that shape them.' And he recounts how, reading as a boy a book published by the Rationalist Press, he found that it had 'just the opposite effect on me to that intended. The christian Scriptures and the catholic rites to which I was accustomed, without losing their wonted sense, gained a quality and a sense of which my pastors and catechisms had told me nothing; a sense of solidarity with creation, with the processes of nature, with the cycles of the seasons. Dramatizations of the processes of vegetation they might be, but had not Christ himself drawn the analogy between the christian self-sacrifice and the grain of wheat which must die if it is to bear fruit? Moreover, these books gave me a new sense of solidarity with humanity as a whole; whatever else I was doing when I attended Mass, or followed the Church's calendar of fast and feast, I was doing something not entirely different from what men and women of every creed and colour seemed to have been doing since the world began.'[1]

Thus at one and the same time the christian finds that he himself is rooted again in Nature and in humanity, and that his religion is rooted in the deepest realities of Nature and humanity and fulfils the secular dreams of humanity and that groaning and travailing of all creation of which St Paul speaks. The christian ritual which might perhaps have seemed to him unreal, unconnected with the realities of everyday life, a relic of an earlier age and a long since outlived view of the universe, is on the contrary revealed precisely in its timelessness, its equal relevance to each and every moment of time, and in its universality, as expressing the yearning, the upward *élan*, of every creature. And the findings of reason, which might

---

[1] *op. cit.* pp. 223-4.

otherwise have seemed to lack conviction no matter how flawless the chain of reasoning, how rigid the logic, now fall into place as part of a total personal certitude, the certitude of a truth which is not only known by the reason but recognized and lived in the deep places of the spirit.

Yet, beyond the way of reason and the way of symbol there is a third way: and it is the deepest, the most incontrovertible, of all. Reason teaches us that God exists, and shows us something of what he is; symbols make us see that the knowledge and love of God are in the deepest sense natural: that life without them is necessarily empty, incoherent, rootless, frustrated; and that if we worship God we worship not as isolated individuals but in company with all mankind and all creation. But if we are to have the complete and utter conviction that transformed the apostles from timid, wavering men into creatures of fire, men whose unstudied eloquence moved the world, we need the kind of knowledge that came to them at Pentecost: we need, not merely to know *about* God, however rich that knowledge may be, but directly to know *God*; we need to go beyond the findings of reason—remembering indeed that even when these reach the sublimity of the speculations of an Aquinas they fall so infinitely far short of the reality of the *mysterium tremendum*, the Infinite Perfect, as to seem but dim adumbrations in comparison with the splendours of even a partial, inchoate vision; we need to go beyond the intimations of Nature, myth and symbol, and launch out into the deep waters of direct communion with God, the ' raising of mind and heart ' to God in prayer.

Here indeed, here above all, the same rhythm of darkness and light, of death and life, is realized. St John of the Cross speaks, in so many words, of the dark night of the senses, the dark night of the soul; but all the great teachers emphasize in one way or another the same essential truth: that you must be prepared to enter into darkness if you would find light, you must be prepared to plunge into the dark cloud of unknowing if you would arrive at vision, you must empty yourself if you would seek infinity, you must be ' stripped and poor and naked ' in your own soul if you would have the kingdom, you must be filled with the sense of your own nothingness before God if you would live within his infinite life:

> ' *To win to the knowledge of all,*
> *Wish not to know anything.*
> *To win to the tasting of all,*
> *Wish not to taste anything.*
> *To come to the possession of all,*
> *Wish not to possess anything.*
> *To win to the being of all,*
> *Wish not to be anything.*'

Those who thus in humble simplicity of heart and in poverty of spirit set themselves to approach God directly, adoring his will and putting their own lives and their own wills into his hands, do indeed achieve a certitude which nothing can shake. It is, then, in helping human beings to achieve this that the supreme task of education lies: a task so immeasurably important that beside it everything else pales into insignificance. Yet to what extent is it attempted? How often people complain that when they were young they were taught to say their prayers indeed, but were never taught how to *pray*, never taught how to be still and *know* the Lord! And yet, as all the saints and mystics tell us, this is no elaborate technical accomplishment: it is the quiet beads of the peasant, the silence of the laysister, the humble soul's simple and perhaps wordless awareness of the indwelling God. Those who achieve it are often far from being clever, far from being learned: but in the end they become wise with a wisdom which the world cannot give; and if they had had no education other than this they would have the ' one thing necessary.' Those who day by day try for a little while to be still and aware of God, who in the simplicities of prayer obey the injunction to be still and know: they come to a knowledge denied to the rest of us, clever and foolish alike. They are not limited to knowledge about God: they know God. They are not limited to a listing of his attributes, nor dismayed by opposition nor put off by paradoxes: for it is God himself who invades and floods their being and transforms them until they see as with his eyes, so that their gaze has his simplicity and, not through knowing so much as through being, they rejoice in a unity and depth of wisdom which though they cannot express it makes all other knowledge seem by comparison negligible. For them no further puzzled questionings, no more agitations of reason: they have plunged into the infinite sea and have found their true element: they are living, at last, in Love. And having come to it through the nothingness and emptiness of selfless humility they find within the Godhead all life and all being: they find not only a new heaven but a new earth; and in the end they can cry with St John of the Cross: ' Mine are the heavens and mine is the earth, mine are mankind and the just and the sinners; the angels are mine and the Mother of God, and all things are mine; and God himself is mine and for me; for Christ is mine and all for me. Truly then, what seekest thou for, my soul, and what does thou ask for? All that is, is thine, and is all for thee.'

IV

The Recovery of Symbol:
The Hero-King

WHEN DR C. G. JUNG, in his *Psychology of the Unconscious,* examines Longfellow's account of the hero Hiawatha—

> ' *How he prayed and how he fasted,*
> *How he lived and toiled and suffered,*
> *That the tribes of men might prosper,*
> *That he might advance his people* '—

he points out that ' we become quickly acquainted with Hiawatha as a saviour and are prepared to hear all that which must be said of a saviour, of his marvellous birth, of his early great deeds, and his sacrifice for his fellow-men.'[1] And so indeed it is: Hiawatha is born of a moon-goddess, his father is the West Wind (*pneuma*); he fights the ' typical battle of the hero for rebirth in the western sea,' a battle in this case with his father (it might be a dragon, a serpent, as indeed later on in the story), which lasts for three whole days; there is then a period of retirement in the forests where he fasts and ' hides himself in the lap of nature,' the womb from which ' it is to be expected that he will emerge again new-born in some form '; this period then leads on to further battles in the dark sea, the waters of death, battles with the serpents and the magician, and so finally the hero departs

> ' *In the glory of the sunset,*
> *In the purple mists of evening,*

[1] *op. cit.* p. 191.

63

The Water and the Fire

To the regions of the home-wind, . . .
To the Islands of the Blessed, . . .
To the land of the Hereafter.'[1]

The story is, in its essentials, to be found repeated again and
again in the myths and legends of the various races of men. Lord
Raglan, in his book *The Hero*, assembles over twenty such stories
and shows how out of their similarities a general sort of 'pattern'
emerges, of which each incident is to be found in the majority of
the stories. Omitting some of these incidents as irrelevant to our
present purpose, we find that the hero's mother is a royal virgin,
his father a king; the circumstances of his conception are unusual,
and he is also reputed to be the son of a god; at birth an attempt
is made to kill him, but he is spirited away, and reared by foster-
parents in a far country. On reaching manhood he returns or goes
to his future kingdom. After a victory over the king and/or a giant,
dragon, or wild beast, he becomes king. Later he is driven from
the throne and city, after which he meets with a mysterious death,
often at the top of a hill. His body is not buried, but nevertheless
he has one or more holy sepulchres.[2]

The similarities with the christian story are obvious: the
virginal conception by the power of the Spirit, the massacre of the
Innocents, the flight into Egypt under the care of the foster-father,
the agony or struggle (*agon*), the way of the Cross, the death on
the hill of Calvary, the empty tomb.

Here then, for the christian, as we saw in the last chapter, is the
sense of solidarity with all humanity and all creation; here too,
more striking even than the similarities, are the essential differences:
the fact that the christian story is set in the most matter-of-fact
everyday world; the fact that the struggle is not an external battle
but an inner agony, that the sacrifice is a self-sacrifice; finally, the
fact that it is not a recurrent ritual but something done once and
for all, something final.

It will be worth our while to dwell a little on the matter-of-
factness of the story, for it is not only essential to the story itself,
it is essential to our response to the story. We are no longer now

[1] *ibid.* pp. 201, 203, 215.
[2] *op. cit.* pp. 178-9. The elements in the pattern-story are given more or less verbatim.

64

in the realm of magic or mere myth; the pattern is something that we have to live ourselves in our own lives; the Cross is life-bringing for us only on condition that we for our part ' take up our (own) cross ' and follow Christ. And all that means something very matter-of-fact for us too.

' If Jesus is the victim of a ritual murder, he is still more obviously the victim of commonplace human passions and vested interests: the jealousy of the clergy, the avarice of Judas, the punctilious conservatism of the Pharisees, the disappointed fury of the revolutionary mob, the appeasement diplomacy of Pilate. If there is a sacrifice, it is now a sordid and secular execution; if there is a labyrinth, it is now the actual winding streets used by the man-in-the-street in a provincial capital; if there is a search, the searcher is now no goddess, but a very human woman called Mary of Magdala, setting about the very human task of embalming a dead human body.'[1]

The search for life is in fact the search for God revealed in Christ; and the story shows us that search, and it is carried out not by a goddess, as when Isis searched for the body of Osiris, but by a woman who is traditionally identified with the woman who was a sinner but of whom the Lord had said that many sins were forgiven her because she had loved much. To embark on the search with hope of success it is not necessary to be a saint: it is necessary only to have a deep sense of one's own sin, to acknowledge and accept one's nothingness, and in humility of heart to be trying to love God. God reveals himself to humanity *in* its squalors; he redeems humanity *in* its squalors.

' A man who is not stripped and poor and naked within his own soul,' writes Fr Thomas Merton, ' will always unconsciously do the works he has to do for his own sake rather than for the glory of God. He will be virtuous not because he loves God's will but because he wants to admire his own virtues. But every moment of the day will bring him some frustration that will make him bitter and impatient, and in his impatience he will be discovered.'[2] So the story begins in a stable: begins in poverty, rejection, dereliction: ' there was no room for them in the inn.' And it is followed

[1] White, *op. cit.* p. 226.   [2] Merton: *Seeds of Contemplation*, ch. IV.

by the flight into Egypt: the 'going out from all things,' the total self-dispossession, the 'self-naughting,' the death of egoism, which alone can reverse the sin of Adam. 'God alone,' says Père Grou, 'has strictly speaking the right to say *I*.'[1] And the *Theologia Germanica* explains that 'it was because of his claiming something for his own, and because of his I, Mine, Me, and the like' that Adam fell, and that we fall in our turn; so that the only way to healing is that 'in me, too, God must be made man; in such sort that God must take to himself all that is in me, within and without, so that there may be nothing in me which striveth against God or hindereth his work.'[2] So it was too that the voice told the Abbot Arsenius: 'Flee, hold thy peace, be still: for these are the roots of sinning not.'[3]

The lesson is reinforced by the mysterious incident of the Finding in the Temple. There are many examples in myth and story of the figure of the *Puer aeternus*, the eternal boy who is the symbol of humanity's longing not merely for immortality but for immortal youth; and he is usually twelve years of age, the apotheosis of childhood before the coming of adolescence; at the same time there are many examples of losing and finding, which is the dying and rising theme under another form. And here in the Gospel story the child is twelve, and is lost and found—and lost for three days—and when he speaks it is of an eternal allegiance that he speaks. It is a mysterious incident because of his apparent harshness, inconsiderateness: 'My Son, why hast thou treated us so? Think, what anguish of mind thy father and I have endured, searching for thee.' And his only reply is to ask them why they should have been troubled: did they not know that he must be with his Father, busied about his Father's concerns?

It is surely a tragedy that we have lost what the primitive Church seems to have had: a devotion precisely to the Boy-Christ. For he should stand, for the christian, not of course for a nostalgic yearning after a vanished youth, nor simply for a longing for an eternal recovery of youth, but again for something very matter-of-fact: for the preservation, or the recovery, here and now of certain

[1] J. Gronu: *Manual*, ch. XXIX.
[2] ch. III (trans. Winkworth).
[3] Cf. Helen Waddell: *The Desert Fathers*, p. 91.

qualities of mind and soul which we associate with childhood, and which are part of the search for God, but which we all too easily lose. St John tells us that ' the Word was made flesh and dwelt amongst us, and we saw his glory, full of grace and truth '; and if we ask why, of all the qualities which would depict the glory, he should single out these two, we may perhaps find an answer if we see in them not only divine life and the revelation of divine truth, but also grace in the sense of graciousness and even gracefulness, and truth in the sense of candour, sincerity, integrity.

For when all due allowance has been made for the debit side, the proclivities towards evil, it remains true that there is about childhood not only the physical grace which artists love to capture in paint and stone, but a certain graciousness of being, something fresh and spontaneous and unspoilt, which can all too quickly disappear as the years go by; and there is a candour and directness, a sincerity and discernment and a hatred of humbug and compromise, which again may easily fail to survive the pressure of the ' common day.' Yet these are qualities which we have to preserve or recover if we are to succeed in our search: for we cannot succeed if we resort to shifts and subterfuges, if we compromise with evil, if we lose all integrity of mind; we can never find our true self if we persist in presenting to the world, and to ourselves, a false self; we can never find God unless we approach God with the simplicity and directness of a child.

But the search *is* a stern and arduous struggle; the self-naughting *is* a sort of death; and perhaps the stern lesson needs to be put sternly if it is really to be brought home to us: it needs to be put with the uncompromising directness of a child. The thing that stands out in the story of the Finding is the sharp contrast between Mary's words, ' thy father and I,' and the Child's reference to his ' Father ' which immediately follows. Later on he is to say, with yet greater apparent harshness, ' If any man come to me, and hate not his father and mother and wife and children and brethren and sisters, yea, and his own life also, he cannot be my disciple ';[1] not of course that we are allowed to have hatred in our hearts for anything, even our enemies, but that nothing, not even the most

[1] *Luke*, xiv, 26.

precious things in life, must be allowed to lead us away from God or to interfere with his service, and that we must be prepared to part with everything, however dear to us, if it would keep us from following Christ. So the *Theologia Germanica* tells us: ' Be simply and wholly bereft of Self.'

So Mary and Joseph, who as yet had not reached a full under- standing of his nature and his mission—they were astonished at the words of Simeon, and here too the words he spoke were ' beyond their understanding '—must come gradually, as Mary ' kept in her heart the memory of all this,' to understand how his love of them cannot but be subordinated to his loyalty to his Father's will, to the work he had to do: and the very sharpness of this first testing will prepare Mary's heart for the ultimate sword.

It is the lesson that has to be learnt by every mother—and every son: the hard lesson that only through separation is meeting possible. If the mother is possessive, ' devouring,' she will never know the real love of a real son; if the son takes refuge from the grimness and dangers and problems of life by retreating again into the mother (his actual mother or some personal or institutional substitute) he will never find his own life or, in consequence, be able to give his own love. He must undertake his own dark journey, and be born anew; only then will he be able really to *meet* his mother: so the Finding in the Temple is followed by the ' separat- ing ' words at Cana, and again during the public ministry—Who is my mother?—and all lead to the final meeting on the road to Calvary with its perfect wordless understanding.[1] So, in the same way, the christian is daily to take up his own cross and undertake his own journey in search of life, in search of God; constantly returning to the ' mother '—the Church, the water, the Spirit—not for refuge and escape but for rebirth and renewal of courage and energy, so as to be liberated from self-centredness and free to busy himself ' about his Father's concerns.'

We in our turn, then, need the figure of the Boy-Christ to remind us that if we hope to find life we must first be ' simply and wholly bereft of self'; to remind us that we shall succeed only if always our first loyalty is to God; to remind us that we need the

[1] Cf. V. White, O.P.: *The Way of the Cross* (Life of the Spirit, April, 1952, p. 412).

integrity and candour of childhood. We need the Child too to remind us that we must have not only integrity of mind but youth-fulness of heart; nothing is easier as life goes on than to grow old in heart, dry and disillusioned and cynical and selfish; nothing is easier than to lose the fire and energy, the ardour and selflessness, the ideals and enthusiasms of youth. We return here to the sense of wonder, for wonder is especially proper to childhood, and it is the sense of wonder above all that keeps us young. But for us human beings the supreme object of wonder, after the Godhead itself, is the glory of the incarnate Word, full of grace and truth; and it is a wonder which, once again, is to be expressed in matter-of-fact terms, in practical loyalty and obedience to Christ's kingship. We too have to be busied at all times with our Father's concerns.

It will be an arduous struggle, as it was for Christ; and it will be an inward struggle, as it was for Christ. But as the hero in the myths, having slain the wild beast, is empowered by putting on the skin of the beast, so we are to be empowered in our weakness by putting on Christ, as St Paul says: receiving, through the Mass and the other sacraments, the divine life and power from him, till we can say, again with St Paul, ' I can do all things in him who strengtheneth me.'

It will be an arduous struggle; for, as the *Theologia Germanica* puts it, ' the life of Christ is every way most bitter to nature and the Self and the Me,' and therefore, ' in each of us, nature hath a horror of it, and thinketh it evil and unjust and a folly, and graspeth after such a life as shall be most comfortable and pleasant to herself, and saith, and believeth also in her blindness, that such a life is the best possible.[1] '

It will be an arduous struggle because it will mean struggling to be poor in spirit: to rid oneself of avarice and greed and possessive-ness: of grasping at things other than God or hankering after them in defiance of the first loyalty; it will mean trying to be contem-plative in regard to things instead of wanting to dominate and master and make everything subservient to one's own pride or profit or pleasure; it will mean learning neither to love things in the wrong way, in defiance of God or apart from God or more

[1] ch. xx.

than God, nor to fail to love them in the right way, to be insensitive and irresponsible instead of loving everything in God and with God and for God; it will mean therefore ' having nothing yet possessing all things'; it will mean being poor in spirit not only about other things but about oneself: recognizing that any gifts that one has come from God and are to be used unselfishly for God and for one's fellow men; it will mean accepting one's own lowliness and weakness and sin; it will mean ceasing to be egocentric and having always one's ' eyes on the Lord'; it will mean learning that other lesson of the *Theologia Germanica*, that a man's highest good is ' that he should not seek himself nor his own things, nor be his own end in any respect, either in things spiritual or things natural, but should seek only the praise and glory of God and his holy will'; for ' nothing burneth in hell but self-will; therefore it hath been said, " Put off thine own will, and there will be no hell." '[1]

It will be an arduous struggle because, in the next place, it will mean trying to be ' clean of heart': to avoid on the one hand the easy declension into sensuality, indolence, a lazy and comfort-loving self-indulgence, and on the other hand a withering of heart, a desiccation and aridity such as may result from a devotion to duty which is not motived by love. It will mean trying to avoid all those vices which destroy the grace and truth we have been considering: the self-deceptions, the twisted vision, the shifts and compromises, the narrow mind and the mean heart which lead to envy and jealousy, the spiteful judgment, the bitterness and intolerance, which poison the soul.

It will be an arduous struggle because it will mean saying, at all times and of all things, all desires, as Christ said in his agony ' Not my will but thine be done': it will mean learning to be, like him, ' obedient unto death, even unto the death of the cross.'

It will be an arduous struggle precisely because it will be a long one, and sooner or later those who attempt it are to expect the coming of that ' noon-day demon' of sloth or accidie, of that tedium or spiritual boredom, of which Cassian wrote with such shrewd insight: ' One gazes anxiously here and there, and sighs

[1] ch. xxxiv.

that no brother of any description is to be seen approaching: one is for ever in and out of one's cell, gazing at the sun as though it were tarrying to its setting: one's mind is in an irrational confusion, like the earth befogged in a mist, one is slothful and vacant in every spiritual activity, and no remedy, it seems, can be found for this state of siege than a visit from some brother, or the solace of sleep. Finally our malady suggests that in common courtesy one should salute the brethren, and visit the sick, near or far. It dictates such offices of duty and piety as to seek out this relative or that, and make haste to visit them . . . : far better to bestow one's pious labour upon these than sit without benefit or profit in one's cell. . . . The blessed Apostle, like a true physician of the spirit . . . busied himself to prevent the malady born of the spirit of accidie. . . . " Study to be quiet . . . and to do your own business . . . and to work with your own hands, as is commended you." '[1]

The unfolding of the story after the Finding seems to emphasize for us the arduous nature of the struggle. The Child's divine sonship and the prior claims of his Father's will once clearly stated, he returns home with his parents and is subject to them (as we in our turn are to be subject to human law and authority and to our human responsibilities within the framework of the eternal law, the will of God); and the rest of his youth is spent in humble, unchronicled retirement, preparing himself for what is to come. And the preparation reaches its climax in his baptism and in the forty days of fasting and prayer alone in the wilderness.

St Thomas, discussing the question whether it was fitting that Christ should be baptized, answers, with Chrysostom, first that he was baptized *non mundari volens, sed mundare aquas*, willing not to be cleansed himself but to cleanse the waters[2], and secondly that though he himself was without sin, he yet took to himself sinful nature and the ' likeness of sinful flesh and of sin: so that though he needed no baptism for himself, yet that carnal nature stood in need of it in others.'[3] And this going down into the waters of rebirth is followed by the retirement into the desert: the final pre-

---

[1] Cf. Helen Waddell: *The Desert Fathers*, pp. 230-1.
[2] *Sum. Theol.* III, xxxix, 1.
[3] *ibid.*

paration, the final gathering of his powers, the final testing, before
he embarks on his public ministry.

It is the climax of the long years of preparation—the thirty
hidden years preparing for the three years of the ministry (for
Jesus was thirty when he began his public life, as was Joseph when
he became governor of the land of Egypt, and David when he
became king, and Ezechiel when he began to prophesy)[1]; and
again and again in the lives of the saints who follow him we find
the same pattern, the initial rebirth in the dark waters, the long
period of silence and retirement, of contemplation and gestation,
before the period of activity in and for the world. Always action,
if it is to be wise, needs the preceding moment of contemplation.
Our Lord does not of course need the self-training any more than
for him the baptism can be a cleansing; yet his human activity, as
human, is built on thought as it is built on his constant prayer to
his Father; and as he prays and groans in spirit before his miracles,
so we may think of him as praying for and thinking over his
ministry, the more so since, as St Thomas points out, quoting
Augustine, 'in this too he would be our mediator, not only by
helping us, but by showing us the way'; and in so doing would
moreover give us confidence in his mercy, for as St Paul says,
'We have not a high priest who can not have compassion on our
infirmities: but one tempted in all things like as we are, without
sin.'[2]

There is of course no question about the reality of our Lord's
temptation. A temptation is a struggle, a battle between two
opposing desires. In Christ there could not be contrariety of will;
there could be, and was, diversity.[3] Just as in the later *agon* in the

---

[1] *Sum. Theol.* III, xxxix, 3.

[2] *Sum. Theol.* III, xli, 1.

[3] *Sum. Theol.* III, xviii, 6. When the senses shrink from pain but the rational will accepts
it, e.g. as necessary for health, there is diversity of wills; there is no contrariety unless the
senses so far prevail as to change or at least hold back the rational will. Thus St Thomas
points out that the human will of Christ did not always will what God willed—an important
fact to remember when considering what the spiritual writers call 'conformity to the will
of God,' for the conformity in fact concerns only the will in its deliberate rational workings.
If the will of God involves pain and death, perfect conformity with it will mean simply
that the rational deliberate choosing of the pain and the death prevail: there will inevitably
be a continuing diversity of wills inasmuch as the senses cannot but shrink from the pain,
and the will in its instinctive workings cannot but shrink from death—the obedience is none
the less perfect for that.

garden his senses could not but recoil from the pain and torment of the Passion, and his will in its natural instinctive workings could not but want to refuse the challenge of death, while on the other hand against these there stood and fought the deliberate choosing of his rational will, his will to do the will of his Father—so that on the one hand he willed to fulfil his love of mankind even to the end, and on the other hand he was tempted, as St Thomas says, to 'sadness, and hatred of mankind'[1]—so also in this first struggle there is a real conflict of desires: and the conflict concerns precisely the nature of his kingship. The rabbinical messianism of the time, which was generally held by the people, believed in the coming of a warrior king who would lead Israel to victory, overthrowing the rule of Rome and gathering together into one kingdom the scattered tribes. Jesus knew this to be the prevalent teaching: he knew that did he but come in power and majesty his success would be immediate and universal. There was surely a great deal to be said for such a plan, as against the failure and folly (and the anguish) of the Cross? The power was his to call upon: why not at least make use of it here alone in the wilderness and turn stones into bread to assuage his hunger? So he would have taken the first step in pride of power, using power idly, unnecessarily, and glorying in it: it would be easy to go on from there till in the end he would have destroyed the whole character of his mission.

Again if he were to throw himself down from the Temple roof and receive no hurt the people would at once acclaim him; and if all the kingdoms of the earth and their glory were at his disposal he would indeed be the Messiah of popular imagination—and humanity would never know the depths of the love and pity of God.[2]

---

[1] *Sum. Theol*, III, xli, 3, ad 3.

[2] A somewhat similar view is to be found in the writings of Solovyev. It is thus summarized by Nadejda Gorodetzky in *The Humiliated Christ in Modern Russian Thought*, pp. 133-4: 'The consciousness of his divine nature and that of the limitations of a natural existence might have induced [Christ] to make his divine power a means for the achievement of something demanded by the state of limitation. For instance, he could make material welfare the aim and divine power a means to obtain it (bread, temptation of the flesh). The divine power could also help in the affirmation of the human personality (" if Thou art the Son "—sin of the reason, pride). Finally, when these lower temptations were eliminated there rose the last, the strongest and worst of all: that of using divine power as violence, even in the name of establishing good. To use divine power for such an aim would be an actual recognition of evil as the main power of the world or, in other words, it would be worship of the principle of evil.' (Cp. also Dostoevsky's Grand Inquisitor.)

The real kingship of Christ is the exact opposite of all this; and the temptation warns us that if we are to accept the kingship, if we are to serve him, it must be in his way and not the way of Satan: it must be in poverty and lowliness of spirit, it must be by an inward transformation, not by a parade of power.

And the same lesson is reinforced when, after the moment of glory, the pageantry and loyalty of Palm Sunday, the agony of the Passion begins. There is first in the garden the agonized cleaving to God in darkness of spirit and ' naked intent of the will ': the moment which is so near to despair, when the soul is weighed down by the feeling of failure and frustration and complete abandonment. There is next the stripping and scourging: and we may think of the stripping away of all self-will in poverty of spirit, and the bearing readily (and if possible gladly) of pain and suffering, as part of our own journey in the steps of Christ. There is the mockery of the crowning, the ultimate humiliation of Christ and the culmination of all his disappointments—the tragedy of ' his own received him not,' of the rich young man whom he loved and who turned from him, of the people of Jerusalem whom he would have gathered ' as the hen doth gather her chickens under her wing,' of the betrayal of Judas and the denials of Peter—and now the acknowledgement of his kingship, his due, turned into cruel mockery: the only coronation he was ever given by men: and we may think of our own small frustrations, humiliations, disappointments, and of how we meet them: self-destructively, with rancour and bitterness and rebellion, or creatively, as part of the process of rebirth.

When we come to the carrying of the cross through the city streets we notice at once the difference between it and the various forms of *transitus* which are to be found in ancient myth. There, it is a question of the triumphant dragging of the slain adversary into a cave and into the waters: here, it is the hero dragging his own weakened body, and the instrument of his own death, to the hill of death, for the sacrificial death is a self-sacrificial death. And when we think of the injunction laid upon us to take up our own cross and follow in our turn, we can find some helpful lessons in the varying attitudes of some of the secondary characters in the story.

74

There is Simon the Cyrenean, of whom we are told that the soldiers forced him to carry the cross: he was far from eager to help, he had to be constrained; but when we think of the woman in the Gospel who touched the hem of Christ's garment and of how he said that virtue, strength, had gone out of him, it is surely legitimate to think that the same thing must have happened to Simon: and that though he began with anger and reluctance to carry the Tree, his journey must have ended in faith and love. And we, though we have no zest for God's service, though we have to force ourselves to it or pray in the words of one of the *Collects* that God may 'compel our rebellious wills': still, if the thing is done in the end we shall gain from it a strengthening of faith and a deepening of love.

Next there are the women in the story, who themselves provide a striking contrast. There are the 'daughters of Jerusalem' who 'bewail and lament him': and they have been plausibly presented by some writers as being far more concerned with their own emotions than with the sufferings of our Lord; indeed it is not they who console him, it is he who is forced to stop and address them. So we are warned against turning religion into a purely emotional thing; a self-centred wallowing in the emotional joys of prayer or 'good works'—*les délices d'une bonne oeuvre*—when these things are made easy would quickly turn into despondency and self-pity and perhaps rebellion the moment they became hard and unrewarding. The love of God has to be something much deeper than that.

Of Mary Magdalen's love there is no question: we have the assurance of Christ himself that much was forgiven her because she loved much. And yet she was to be told later on in the garden of resurrection, 'Do not cling to me': do not be possessive, and do not think that the time is now come for carefree joy: there is still work to be done. Her love, in other words, fierce though it is, is still at this stage imperfect, still too predominantly emotional, insufficiently selfless. The lesson is doubly consoling for us: even though love is imperfect, still much will be forgiven on account of it; and on the other hand, because love is not essentially a question of feelings but of will, those who cannot feel much eagerness or joy in God's service are not to be discouraged: to will to serve him is all he asks.

Then, finally, his mother. She loves him with her body, with all the feeling that is in her, with all her heart; she loves him with the utterly selfless will-to-help—to pour into his heart her strength and comfort—which is the essence of love. So she will stand, silent and rigid, at the side of the cross, a pillar of strength to help him; she will not weep, for tears would only add to his sufferings: there will be time for that when she takes his body into her arms. She is the embodiment of the perfection of human love in its blending of strength and tenderness.

If God, then, gives an emotional joy in his service it must be recognized for what it is, a gift, and used as it is meant to be used: in the forming of a habit of ready obedience which will lead to the other, deeper love which moods and feelings cannot lessen nor crosses destroy. And once again we return to the matter-of-factness both of the Passion story and of the response to it demanded of us: that love means sharing and helping; that we are to shoulder our own cross whatever it may be with as little concern as possible and with no self-pity, devoting ourselves on the contrary to doing what we can to help others with theirs.

The story goes on to its climax: the Crucifix is raised, the Tree is planted in the ground; there is darkness 'over all the earth,' and out of the darkness comes the cry of dereliction—no longer, as Solovyev notes, the 'Father' of Christ's personal prayer, but the voice of all creation in its travail, 'My God, my God.'[1]

This moment of darkness and death is the supreme—and supremely efficacious—symbol of that self-naughting in which alone, all the wise men tell us, we can find the way to life. In the beginning of time the Spirit brooded over the dark waters of chaos and light was born; and here at the central point of human history it is in darkness that the world is reborn; and always to those who are 'born again of water and the spirit' it is in darkness that the Spirit comes. So the cosmic rhythm, the pattern of the myths, the dreams of humanity, are fulfilled. For unless there is the darkness

---

[1] Cf. Gorodetzky, *op. cit.* p. 134.

and the death the soul will not be 'stripped and poor and naked' and will oppose the entry of life.

For us, the darkness may assume many different forms. It may be the loss of hard-won worldly possessions and security, the collapse of a carefully built-up career; it may be the loss of another human being without whom life is meaningless; it may be the loss of health or sight or hearing; it may be an agony of physical pain or mental suffering; it may be a collapse of what had seemed a well-ordered moral life, or the apparent loss of what had hitherto been a firm, unquestioning faith; it may be the Dark Nights of St John of the Cross, or something resembling them. Or it may be, not some abyss of darkness into which we are hurled by events which are none of our choosing, but a darkness to which we bring ourselves through deepening self-knowledge: the sense of our own sin, the evil that holds us in thrall, our own meanness, hypocrisy, unreality. It may begin with something very like the noon-day demon of Abbot Cassian: a *taedium vitae*, an unbearable fatigue of spirit—'Heavy is God's plough for tired hands 'wrote the Russian thinker Tareev, which nothing seems capable of conquering. It may be a complete desolation of spirit, a near-despair, a feeling as it were of solidarity with the 'lost people,' a descent into hell. . . .

This last agony also Christ took upon himself, if we are to believe such writers as William Law, for whom Christ's greatest suffering was his 'second death,' his entry into the eternal death which was fallen man's fate: an agony which, he says, begins with the cry, 'My soul is sorrowful,' and continues to the final dereliction of the *Eloi, Eloi, lama sabachthani*: an entry into the last terrors of the lost soul, 'feeling, bearing, and overcoming the pains and darkness of that eternal death which the fallen soul of Adam had brought into it,' so that no other might suffer it.[1]

But the *Theologia Germanica* tells us: 'Christ's soul must needs descend into hell before it ascended into heaven. So must also the soul of man. But mark ye in what manner this cometh to pass. When a man truly perceiveth and considereth himself utterly vile and wicked, and unworthy of all the comfort and kindness that he hath ever received from God, or from the creatures, he

[1] W. Law: *Selected Mystical Writings*, ed. Hobhouse, pp. 61-2.

falleth into such a deep abasement and despising of himself, that he thinketh himself unworthy that the earth should bear him, and it seemeth to him reasonable that all creatures in heaven and earth should rise up against him. . . . And it seemeth to him that he shall be eternally lost and damned, and a footstool to all the devils in hell, . . . but he is willing to be unconsoled and unreleased, and he doth not grieve over his condemnation and sufferings; for they are right and just . . . and he hath nothing to say against them. Nothing grieveth him but his own guilt and wickedness; for that is not right and is contrary to God, and for that cause he is grieved and troubled in spirit. This is what is meant by true repentance for sin. And he who in this present time entereth into this hell, entereth afterward into the Kingdom of Heaven, and obtaineth a foretaste thereof which excelleth all the delight and joy which he ever hath had or could have in this present time from temporal things.'[1]

It is in a similar sense that we are to understand the oft-repeated phrase of the Russian *staretz* Silouan—the reply given him by God when he prayed for the grace to grow humble: ' Keep thy mind in hell, and despair not.' To do so is indeed to be ' stripped and poor and naked '; and so it is that the *Theologia* goes on to tell us that ' God hath not forsaken a man in this hell, but is laying his hand upon him ' that he may be made a partaker ' of all manner of joy, bliss, peace, rest and consolation.'[2] So the psalmist, writing of a caravan of pilgrims to the holy city, describes how ' as they journey through the arid valley they change it into a place full of springs, yea, a place of blessings it becomes under the autumn rains: they march on from strength to strength; they appear before God in Zion.'[3] The soul of man must cry his *De profundis* before he can sing his *Gloria in excelsis*; but if he uses the darkness, whatever form it may take, thus creatively to rid himself of all his unrealities, his pride and his pretences, his meannesses and self-will, his sloth and his shallowness, and stands naked before God, prepared at last to accept his kingship, prepared at last to say ' Not my

[1] *Theol. Germ.*, ch. XI.
[2] *loc. cit.*
[3] Ps. 83 according to the meaning of the Hebrew : the sense of the Vulgate version is different in these verses.

will but thine be done,' then the infinite life will flood into him, he will be reborn, and out of the darkness will come a great light, and the desert will become a place full of springs.

My kingship, our Lord said, is not of this world. The true crowning of his humanity by man is to be done inwardly in the hearts of men. And when he is thus enthroned in a human heart which has known the darkness and has faced it creatively and now knows and lives in the light, it is impossible for that heart to grow old and dry and cynical and self-absorbed: it must become a place full of springs: it must have in it the ardour and high purpose, the freshness and energy, of unspoilt youth, because it is living in love, and love is always pouring into it, and so it becomes in truth an *organum pulsatum a Spiritu sancto*, an instrument played on by the holy Spirit, empowered by Christ as the hero was empowered by putting on the skin of the slain animal, and so, able at all times, whatever the moment may bring, to co-operate with the work of the Spirit in renewing, rejuvenating, the face of the earth.

V

The Recovery of Symbol:
The Fire of Life

'OUR GOD,' says the *Epistle to the Hebrews*, 'is a consuming Fire.'[1] The words are immediately an echo of a verse in the book of *Deuteronomy*; but they also echo the voice of humanity as a whole. Every year, on the night preceding Easter morning, the Church celebrates the making and blessing of the New Fire; and this too finds its parallels or adumbrations in primitive fire-producing rites all over the world.[2]

Dr Jung, in his *Psychology of the Unconscious*, has gathered numerous examples of such rites and, bringing his immense philological erudition to his aid, has discussed their significance. That the symbolism is sexual is clear; but the sexual itself is symbolic of something further and greater: behind the individual procreative libido is the universal creative Spirit: the fire is the ' treasure difficult to attain,' the fire-bringer is the Mediator, and we find ourselves again in the sphere of redemption and rebirth.

If such a juxtaposition of the sexual and the sacred disturbs us (and, as we shall see, the Church has no such inhibitions) it is because in our attitude to sex we have lost an insight—which primitive man possesses—of fundamental importance: the awareness of what Prof. Mircea Eliade calls the *sacralité de la sexualité*, the idea of

[1] *Hebr.* xii, 29.

[2] If the main theme of this book is valid, we must certainly see as a happy augury for the future the fact that the Church has chosen this moment to restore these rites to their proper setting in the darkness of night, i.e. to restore their full richness and significance as symbols.

sexuality as the 'direct manifestation of the sacred in the life of the cosmos.' For primitive man, he writes, 'sexuality always bears a cosmological significance, and by that very fact is in some sense made symbolic, trans-substantialised. . . . For such a man there is no such thing as sexual life in its 'pure' state, exempt from all symbolic implications. Even when the sexual act is not formulated in cosmological terms, i.e. when it is not clearly identified with a *hierosgamos*, a sacred marriage, it is none the less charged with religious symbolism . . . [and] assimilated to all the other cosmic forces which periodically regenerate the world. It is thanks to its sacred character that the orgy plays so important a role in the festivals of vegetation and especially in the decisive moments of the agricultural cycle (seed-time, germination, harvest). All the excesses of an unleashed collective sexuality are explained by the assimilation of the sexual act to the union of Heaven with the Earth-Mother: a mystical solidarity binds together all the creative energies which vivify and renew the cosmos.'[1]

Fire, then, is the new life; the fire-bringer is the Mediator, bringing the life from heaven to earth. Dr Jung notes, for example: 'The Sanskrit word for fire is *agnis* (the Latin *ignis*); the fire personified is the god Agni, the divine mediator, whose symbol has certain points of contact with that of Christ. In Avesta and in the Vedas the fire is the messenger of the gods. In the christian mythology certain parts are closely related with the myth of Agni.' And alluding to the story in the book of *Daniel* of how the king Nebuchadnezzar, having thrown the three men into the fiery furnace, cried with amazement: 'Behold, I see four men loose, walking in the midst of the fire, and there is no hurt in them, and the form of the fourth is like the Son of God,' he notes that, according to a mystical interpretation, the story 'appears as a magic fire ceremony by means of which the Son of God reveals himself. . . . The glowing furnace (like the glowing tripod in "Faust") is a mother symbol, where the children are produced. The fourth in the fiery furnace appears as Christ, the Son of God, who has become a visible God in the fire. . . . It is said of the Saviour of Israel (the

[1] Cf. *Chasteté, Sexualité et Vie Mystique chez les Primitifs*, in *Mystique et Continence* (Etudes Carmélitaines, 1952).

Messiah) and of his enemies, *Isaiah* x, 17: " And the light of Israel shall be for a fire, and his Holy One for a flame." In a hymn of the Syrian Ephrem it is said of Christ: " Thou who art all fire, have mercy upon me." '[1]

Elsewhere also in the Old Testament it is through fire that the divine presence is manifested: in the burning bush, the pillar of fire which was with the Israelites in the desert, the flame and smoke on Sinai, the visions of Ezechiel. So too the divine Wisdom says to St Catherine of Siena, ' I am Fire, the acceptor of sacrifices'; and Pascal, searching for words to express his experience of ' The God of Abraham, the God of Isaac, the God of Jacob,' could find only the one word, ' Fire.'

But the fire-bringer is especially the Mediator: the re-creative Sun-God. ' Every morning a god-hero is born from the sea; he mounts the chariot of the sun. In the west a great mother awaits him and he is devoured by her in the evening. In the belly of a dragon he traverses the depths of the midnight sea. After a frightful combat with the serpent of night he is born again in the morning.[2]'
' The sun, victoriously arising, tears itself away from the embrace and clasp, from the enveloping womb of the sea, and sinks again into the maternal sea, into night, the all-enveloping and the all-reproducing, leaving behind it the heights of midday and all its glorious works. This image was . . . profoundly entitled to become the symbolic carrier of human destiny; in the morning of life man painfully tears himself loose from the mother, from the domestic hearth, to rise through battle to his heights. . . . His life is a constant struggle with death . . . [but] this death is no external enemy, but a deep personal longing for quiet and for the profound peace of non-existence, for a dreamless sleep in the ebb and flow of the sea of life. Even in his highest endeavour for harmony and equilibrium, for philosophic depths and artistic enthusiasm, he seeks death, immobility, satiety and rest. . . . If he is to live he must fight and sacrifice his longing for the past, in order to rise to his own heights. And having reached the noonday heights, he must also *sacrifice the love of his own achievement*, for he may not loiter.

[1] *op. cit.* pp. 101-2.
[2] C. G. Jung: *Contributions to Analytical Psychology*, p. 112.

The sun also sacrifices its greatest strength in order to hasten onwards to the fruits of autumn, which are the seeds of immortality; fulfilled in children, in works, in posthumous fame, in a new order of things.'[1]

Not to will satiety and rest (death: retreat from reality, i.e. retreat from Reality, from God, into the comfort of the false Adam-self;) but to achieve, and then to sacrifice the love of the achievement. Let us set beside this quotation from Jung a passage from the *Theologia Germanica*: 'All that in Adam fell and died, was raised again and made alive in Christ, and all that rose up and was made alive in Adam, fell and died in Christ. But what was that? I answer, true obedience and disobedience. But what is true obedience? I answer, that a man should so stand free, being quit of himself, that is, of his I, and Me, and Self, and Mine, and the like, that in all things, he should no more seek or regard himself, than if he did not exist, and should take as little account of himself as if he were not, and another had done all his works. . . . And this obedience fell and died in Adam, and rose again and lived in Christ. Yes, Christ's human nature was so utterly bereft of Self, and apart from all creatures, as no man's ever was, and was nothing else but " a house and habitation of God." Neither of that in him which belonged to God, nor of that which was a living human nature and a habitation of God, did he, as man, claim anything for his his own. His human nature did not even take unto itself the Godhead, whose dwelling it was, nor anything that this same Godhead willed, or did or left undone in him, nor yet anything of all that his human nature did or suffered; but in Christ's human nature there was no claiming of anything, nor seeking nor desire, saving that what was due might be rendered to the Godhead, and he did not call this very desire his own.'[2]

The sun-god, the wanderer, dying and rising, is at one and the same time ' the sacrificial flame, the sacrificer, and the sacrificed, as Christ himself.'[3] It is not surprising then that we find in the christian liturgy that Christ is referred to as the New Sun, the Sun of Salvation, as Light and Life, the Builder of the world, or that

---

[1] C. G. Jung: *Psychology of the Unconscious*, p. 215.
[2] ch. xv.
[3] C. G. Jung: *op. cit.* p. 102.

to him are applied the words of Malachi, ' Unto you . . . the Sun of justice shall arise, and health in his wings.'[1]

But ' our God is a consuming Fire '; and the same prophet Malachi asks concerning the ' day of his coming ': ' Who shall stand to see him? for he is like a refining fire . . . and he shall purify the sons of Levi, and shall refine them as gold and as silver.'[2] There is to be an identification in some sense, and a real, inner identification between the God redeeming and man redeemed; but it can only be at the cost of a radical purification, it can only be ' yet so as by fire.' The identification itself is clearly expressed in the writings of the mystics.[3]

' Mechtild of Magdeburg, and after her Dante, saw Deity as a flame or river of fire that filled the Universe; and the " deified " souls of the saints as ardent sparks therein, ablaze with that fire, one thing with it, yet distinct. Ruysbroeck, too, saw " Every soul like a live coal, burned up by God on the heart of his infinite Love." Such fire imagery has seemed to many of the mystics a peculiarly exact and suggestive symbol of the transcendent state which they are struggling to describe.'[4] So Boehme pictures the soul in this state under the likeness of a ' bright flaming piece of iron ' so penetrated by the fire which shines through it that ' it giveth light '; and five centuries earlier, Richard of St Victor used the same imagery: ' " When the soul is plunged in the fire of divine love," he says, " like iron, it first loses its blackness, and then growing to white heat, it becomes like unto the fire itself. And lastly, it grows liquid, and losing its nature is transmuted into an utterly different quality of being." " As the difference between iron that is cold and iron that is hot," he says again, " so is the difference between . . . the tepid soul and the soul made incandescent by divine love." '[5] And Ruysbroeck again describes how, when men have thus reached the

[1] iv, 2.
[2] iii, 2-3.
[3] The christian mystics of course make no claim to ontological identity between the human personality and God; even though they speak of ' deification ' they are at pains to point out that the personality remains intact, indeed more real than before, but that what takes place is, as Evelyn Underhill expresses it, a ' transfusion of their selves ' by God's self, ' an entrance upon a new order of life, so high and so harmonious with Reality that it can only be called divine.'
[4] E. Underhill: *Mysticism*, pp. 420-1.
[5] *ibid.* p. 421.

' summit of their spirits,' ' their bare understanding is drenched
through by the Eternal Brightness, even as the air is drenched
through by the sunshine. And the bare, uplifted will is transformed
and drenched through by abysmal love, even as iron is by fire.'[1]

For St John of the Cross, similarly, the holy Spirit is a ' living
flame of love ': and ' this flame the soul feels within it, not only
as a fire that has consumed and transformed it in sweet love, but
also as a fire which burns within it and sends out flame,' and the
flame ' bathes the soul in glory and refreshes it with the temper of
divine life. . . . Wherefore the soul that is in a state of transformation
of love may be said to be, in its ordinary habit, like to the log of
wood that is continually assailed by the fire; and the acts of this
soul are the flame that arises from the fire of love: the more intense
is the fire of union, the more vehemently does the flame issue forth.
. . . And it is a wondrous thing, worthy to be related, that, though
this fire of God is so vehement and so consuming that it would
consume a thousand worlds more easily than natural fire consumes
a straw of flax, it consumes not the spirits wherein it burns, neither
destroys them; but rather, in proportion to its strength and heat, it
delights them and deifies them, burning sweetly in them by reason
of the purity of their spirits. Thus it came to pass . . . when this
fire descended with great vehemence and enkindled the disciples
and, as St Gregory says, they burned inwardly with sweetness. And
it is this that the Church says, in these words: There came fire
from heaven, burning not but giving splendour, consuming not
but enlightening.'[2]

St John goes on to describe how this same divine fire ' wounds
the soul with the tenderness of the life of God; and so deeply and
profoundly does it wound it and fill it with tenderness that it causes
it to melt in love, so that there may be fulfilled in it that which
came to pass to the Bride in the *Song of Songs*. . . When the Spouse
spake, my soul melted '; and he applies to this wounding which is
' the office of love . . . that it may enkindle with love and cause
delight ' the words with which the book of *Proverbs* describes the
' playing of God ': ' I was delighted every day as I played before

[1] E. Underhill: *Mysticism*, p. 422.
[2] *Living Flame of Love*, edit. E. Allison Peers, pp. 20-21, 41.

him alway, playing over the whole earth, and my delight is to be with the sons of men, namely, by giving myself to them.'[1]

But before this ' feast of the holy Spirit takes place in the substance of the soul,' the soul must first lose its blackness: the dross must be burned away, and it is here that the fire is indeed a consuming fire. ' For the same fire of love which afterwards is united with the soul and glorifies it is that which aforetime assailed it in order to purge it; even as the fire which penetrates the log of wood is the same that first attacked and wounded it with its flame, cleansing and stripping it of all its accidents of ugliness, until, by means of its heat, it had prepared it to such a degree that it could enter it and transform it into itself.' It is here that the ' soul endures great suffering,' for in this stage the fire ' is not bright to it, but dark . . . not delectable to it, but arid . . . nor is there any thought that can console it, nor can it raise its heart to God, since this flame has become so oppressive to it '; and St John quotes the words of Jeremiah, that God ' hath brought me into darkness and not into light; so greatly is he turned against me and turneth his hand. He hath made my skin and my flesh to grow old and hath broken my bones; he hath builded a wall round about me and hath encompassed me with gall and travail. He hath set me in dark places as those that are dead for ever.'[2] This ' image of the divine vitality successively experienced as a painful Fire and a heavenly Light—of the purging of the soul as in a furnace; the anguish through which it passes to that condition of harmony in which, " itself becoming fire," the flame that has been in its onslaught a torment to the separated will becomes to the transmuted creature an indwelling radiance, a source of joy and life—all this is found again and again in the later christian mystics. . . . " As a bar of iron, heated red-hot, becomes like fire itself, forgetting its own nature," says St Bernard, . . . so in the saints all human affections melt away, by some unspeakable transmutation, into the will of God." " The naked will," says Ruysbroeck, " is transformed by the Eternal Love as fire by fire." " We are like coals," he says in another

---

[1] *op. cit.* p. 23.
[2] St John of the Cross, *op. cit.* pp. 28-29. The ' dark fire' in St John's sense must not of course be confused with William Law's ' dark fire-breath ' which is alluded to below p. 87.

place, " burned on the hearth of Infinite Love." '[1] And St Catherine of Genoa describes how ' this holy soul, yet in the flesh, found herself placed in the purgatory of God's burning love, which consumed and purified her from whatever she had to purify, in order that after passing out of this life she might enter at once into the immediate presence of God her Love.'[2]

Just as the sun is at one and same time the beneficent life-bringer, the youthful god who gives light and warmth and fecundity, and the terrible scorching death-bringer; so the divine Sun is both heavenly radiance of light and painful, consuming Fire. Some of the mystics have described the soul in terms of a similar ambivalence. So for William Law all life is fire; but the soul remains a dark fire-breath, an anger-fire, until it is born again into the true image of God through repentance. But no repentance is possible unless we *see* this deformity and are terrified at it: we cannot be truly religious if we have only known the ' want of a Saviour by hearsay '; so with Christ we must cross the brook Cedron and sweat drops of sorrow. The temptation, he goes on, is to keep all things quiet in us (Jung's ' deep personal longing for quiet and for the profound peace of non-existence ') by outward forms and modes of religion, or by the comforts, cares and delights of the world; but a Redeemer is given us to quench the wrath which stands between us and God—a wrath which is not his own but ' what is awakened in the dark fire of our own fallen nature ': only our own will separates us, whereby we live to ourselves (Jung's ' love of one's own achievement '); it is that self that Christ calls on us to deny, to hate and to lose. ' Thus strength and fire in the divine nature are nothing else but the strength and flame of love, and never can be anything else; but in the creature strength and fire may be separated from love, and then they become an evil, they are wrath and darkness and all mischief.' For fire is ' merely a desire . . . which is its own kindler,' and ' what our desire kindles, that becomes the fire of our own life, and fits us

---

[1] E. Underhill: *The Mystic Way*, pp. 324-5. Cp. Walter Hilton: ' On the self wise it is said that God is fire: *Deus noster ignis consumens est* . . . For as fire wasteth all bodily thing that may be wasted, right so the love of God burneth and wasteth all sin out of the soul and maketh it clean, as fire maketh clean all manner metal.' (*Scale of Perfection*, Book II, ch. xxxiii.)

[2] Underhill: *op. cit.* p. 325.

either for the majestic glories of the kingdom of God, or the dark horrors of hell.'[1]

The soul is feminine to God. In all these testimonies of the mystics it is God who purifies, the soul which is purified, for we are not 'sufficient to think any thing of ourselves, as of ourselves, but our sufficiency is from God.'[2] There is of course all the labour, the arduous struggle, of asceticism: without that primary 'active purification' there could never be the 'passive purification' which is God's ultimate drawing of the personality into union with himself—the iron finally made incandescent by the Fire. But just as we shall never understand, still less achieve, holiness if we think of it in terms of self-achieved 'character,' so we shall never understand the process of purifying and rebirth if we think of it or of any part of it, active or passive, as something we can do of ourselves. The effort, the energy, the ardour, whether in doing or in suffering must come from us: the power can only come from God, from the divine Mediator. The fire is brought to us, no longer in 'mere myth' as with Prometheus, the 'Robber' who stole the fire from the gods, but in real and efficacious fact by Christ who 'being in the form of God, thought it not robbery to be equal to God, but emptied himself, taking the form of a servant . . . [and] humbled himself, becoming obedient unto death. . . . For which cause God also hath exalted him. . . . Wherefore, my dearly beloved . . . with fear and trembling work out your salvation, for it is God who worketh in you, both to will and to accomplish.'[3]

The fire is brought to us, the life is brought to us, through the Mediator, by the Spirit, using the instrumentality of baptism and the other sacraments. Calvary is consummated in Pentecost; and thereafter through the ages the continuing sacrifice of the Son is consummated for us in the continuing coming and indwelling of the Spirit in sacramental life and sanctifying grace. So Christ speaks of his death on the Cross, the tree of death which is also the tree of life, the instrument of universal rebirth, as a baptism:

[1] *op. cit.* pp. 11 seq., 39, 50-52.
[2] *II Cor.* iii, 5.
[3] *Phil.* ii, 6-13.

'I have a baptism to be baptized with; and how am I straitened until it be accomplished!'[1]

And so we return to the liturgy of Holy Saturday Night, in which the fire is made and blessed, the baptismal water is sanctified, and baptism is given.[2]

The ritual of the blessing of the new fire itself is very simple: the fire is to be struck from a flint outside the church and charcoal is lighted from it; then the fire is blessed with a simple prayer: 'O God, who through thy Son, the Corner-Stone, hast kindled in the faithful the fire of thy brightness, deign to sanctify unto our profit this fire struck from the flint; and grant us, by this paschal festival, to be so inflamed with heavenly desire that we may in the end come purified in mind to the feast of never-ending light, through the same Christ our Lord.'[3]

There follows the blessing of the Paschal Candle; and the deacon sings the *Exultet*, the Easter hymn of praise:

Exult, ye heavenly hosts, proclaim these mysteries divine;
Sound forth, ye trumpets of salvation, the victory of so great a King.
Rejoice, O earth, made radiant by such splendour:
Your darkness flown, the King's eternal brightness be your light . . .

This is the night in which our forefathers, Israel's sons,
Were led forth from out of Egypt's yoke
Dryshod through the Red Sea to their liberty.
This night dispelled sin's darkness by a pillar of fire.
This is the night when now o'er the earth are freed
Christ's followers from vices of the world . . .
This is the night when Christ burst through the bonds of death
And rose victorious from the nether world . . .
O happy fault which merited for us
A Saviour so worthy and so great!

[1] *Luke*, xii, 50.

[2] In the early Church, the baptism of adults was kept to this particular night of the year, and even now the Roman Ritual recommends that it be celebrated either on this night or on the vigil of Pentecost (which ends the Easter season).

[3] Cf. Philip T. Weller: *The New Easter Vigil Service*, from which all the translations of this liturgy here quoted are taken, with slight modifications.

O truly blessed night, which alone deserved to know
The time and hour when Christ arose from hell !
This is the night of which it was written:
The night shall be enlightened as the day,
The night to be my light in my delights.
The holiness of this night banishes crime,
Cleanses from sin, restores innocence to fallen man,
And brings back gladness to sorrowing humanity.
This is the night bringing enmity to naught,
Inspiring peace among nations, and humbling the mighty.

Accept, then, holy Father, for the sake of this night
Our evening offering of this sacred flame . . .
This waxen light, the handiwork of bees . . .

O night when heaven is joined to earth and God to man !
We beseech thee, therefore, O Lord, that this candle, consecrated to the
*   honour of thy name,*
May continue burning, and scatter this night's gloom . . .
And may it mingle with the stars on high;
May the Morning Star find its flame aglow—
That light-bearing Star which knows no setting,
That star which is Christ, who, risen from the tomb,
Shines down on humankind in serene light . . .'

Now the ' Prophecies ' are read: passages from the Old Testament which foreshadow the events of the New Covenant: the story of creation (followed by the prayer, ' O God, who in wondrous manner created man, but still more wonderfully redeemed him '); the delivery from the Egyptian bondage through the waters of the Red Sea; the passage from *Isaiah* (iv. 1-6) which speaks of God's purifying of Israel by water and by fire; and finally, the verses from *Deuteronomy* (iv), in which Moses warns his people against obstinacy and infidelity to the light.

Next, after the litany has been sung, there follows the blessing of the baptismal font: the priest prays to God to ' send forth the spirit of adoption to beget new life in them that are born unto thee in this font of baptism': and begs that he may 'render this water fruitful for giving rebirth to mankind, that whosoever is sanctified in the stainless womb of this font may be born again as a new creature, and come forth as an offspring of heaven'; he prays that the water may 'become a living fountain, a water that regenerates, a stream that purifies.' He then breathes upon it in the form of a cross, praying: 'Do thou bless with thy mouth these pure waters, that, besides their natural power for the cleansing of the body, they may also be effectual for the purifying of the soul.' Now he plunges the paschal candle into the water, and again breathes on it in the form of the Greek letter *psi* which is the initial letter of the word for spirit or life-giving principle, and prays that the power of the holy Spirit may descend into the deepest being of the water and make its whole substance fruitful for bestowing spiritual rebirth. Oil and chrism are then poured into the water, and the final blessing invoked; the baptisms follow.[1] There is finally the singing of *Psalm* 41: 'As the hart panteth after the fountains of water, so doth my soul long for thee, O God,' and a concluding prayer for the sanctification of both soul and body.

So, for the christian, the secular dream, the universal myth, of humanity is fulfilled: the rebirth through the water, the rebirth through the fire. In considering the myth of the hero-king we saw that the birth of the hero is in some way or another strange and mysterious; and the reason is that, as Dr Jung remarks, 'the birth

---

[1] The rite of baptism itself is of course full of richly significant symbolism; and could thus provide a lesson—rather, a forming and training of the personality—of priceless value for the christian. What a tragedy that it has become an obscure private ceremony, attended only by those immediately concerned, so that many christians remain perforce virtually unacquainted with it and its vital significance. The instructions for the revised Easter Vigil liturgy direct that the blessing of the font and the baptisms should be followed by the renewal of baptismal vows by all the faithful present: what a magnificent thing it would be if baptism became again, in every parish, the most important ritual event, after the Mass, in the life of the parish as a whole, as a family! Surely things could be so arranged that, once a month let us say, baptism formed the major part of the evening service on Sunday: carried out with full solemnity and, except for the essential words of the baptismal formula, spoken clearly in the vernacular so that its lessons (which nowadays no doubt would need first of all to be explained in detail to the people, perhaps in a series of preliminary sermons) should sink deeply into the souls of all present: this could be followed by the renewal of baptismal vows as on Holy Saturday; and the service could end with a short Benediction: so the people would have, brought home to them in a form which goes deeper than words, the central facts of the christian life—the rebirth and all that it implies, and the abiding sacramental Presence. But as things are, all this is normally lost to the christian: what an appalling waste!

of the hero, as a rule, is not that of an ordinary mortal, but is a rebirth from the mother-spouse; hence it occurs under mysterious ceremonies'; and he goes on to note that the twofold birth 'has attained a lofty significance in the christian mythology': in Christ, as 'rebirth through the second mother, the mysterious tree of death,' so that, as we have seen, Christ speaks of his death as a baptism, 'he interprets his death agony symbolically as birth agony'; and in the christian, through baptism itself 'which, as we have seen, represents rebirth. Thus man is born not merely in a commonplace manner, but also born again in a mysterious manner, by means of which he becomes a participator of the kingdom of God, of immortality. Anyone may become a hero in this way who is generated anew through his own mother, because only through her does he share in immortality.'[1]

So, as he also notes elsewhere, in the mystery of baptism, 'Christ is the bridegroom; the church is the bride; the baptismal font is the womb of the church, as it is still called in the text of the *Benedictio fontis*. The holy water has salt put into it—with the idea of fertilization or making it like the sea. A *hierosgamos* or holy wedding is celebrated on the holy Sabbath in the service just mentioned, and a burning candle as a phallic symbol is plunged three times into the font, in order to fertilize the baptismal water and lend it the qualities necessary to give a new birth to the child baptized (*quasi modo genitus*). The *mana* personality, the medicine man, is the *pontifex maximus*, the Papa; the church is the *mater ecclesia*, the *magna mater*, and mankind the helpless children needing grace.' And he goes on, still speaking of course strictly from the point of view, and within the terms of reference, of the scientific psychologist, to point out how these images (again from the psychological point of view: the data do not of themselves admit of the formulation of any metaphysical or theological conclusions) 'permit the catholic to experience a considerable portion of his collective unconscious in tangible reality. He has no need to go in quest of some authority, or superior power, some revelation, or connexion with the eternal and the timeless, [for] these are always present and available for him. In the sacred precincts of every altar

[1] *Psychology of the Unconscious*, p. 196.

for him there dwells a god. It is the Protestant and the Jew who have to seek; for the one has, in a sense, destroyed the earthly body of the godhead, and the other has never found it.'[1]

For the christian, the dream is fulfilled and is no longer a dream; the myth is no longer mere myth. The fire is become the reality of the indwelling and purifying Spirit; the water is, not in figure merely but in realized fact, a 'fountain springing up into life everlasting.'[2]

But all this, as we have seen, is something which, no longer to be acted but to be lived, must be accomplished inwardly as a transmutation of the personality. And first there is the process, described by St Catherine of Genoa in the words already quoted, of the soul who, while 'yet in the flesh, found herself placed in the purgatory of God's burning love, which consumed and purified her from whatever she had to purify.' Where this process is left uncompleted in this life it is completed, according to the doctrine of the same saint, in a precisely similar way in the next life: 'The souls are covered with a rust, the rust of sin, which is gradually burned away by the fire of purgatory. The more it is burned away, the more they respond to God their true Sun: their happiness increases as the rust falls off, and lays them open to the divine Light.'[3] The fire is willingly, nay, eagerly sought; as in the words of Gerontius:

> ' Take me away; and in the lowest deep
> There let me be;'

and as the process of purification goes on the anguish turns more and more into joy; which explains why purgatory is traditionally pictured, now as a place of torment, now, as in St Bede the Venerable, as a flowery meadow so gay and beautiful that the visionary took it to be heaven. The same is true of the earthly purgation: just as in general the 'spiritual life has a rhythm,' as Berdyaev noted, ' its intensity should seek relief in repose, its suffering in joy, its tears in laughter. Laughter is an independent spiritual problem

---

[1] *Contributions to Analytical Psychology*, pp. 115-6.
[2] *John*, iv, 14.
[3] Cf. E. Underhill: *The Mystic Way*, p. 325.

which has been little investigated. Laughter has a liberating quality which exalts man above his daily worries and oppressive suffering '[1]; so also in the deep waters of the mystical life there is the same mixture of joy and sorrow, of pain and ecstasy, until, as the consummation of the process draws near, sorrow is more and more turned into joy—not succeeded *by* joy, but transmuted by love *into* joy.

But purgation is but one aspect of the process. The rust is burned away; but also the iron becomes gradually incandescent. The saints are depicted with a halo—it is a sun-symbol—because they have ' become fire ': they are living the life of the Spirit in its fullness: they are living fully and wholly in love.

They are living in love because they are wholly possessed by love, by the Spirit-Fire. ' It is expedient to you that I go,' Christ told his disciples, ' for if I go not, the Paraclete will not come to you; but if I go, I will send him to you.'[2] The incarnate Word must first go, must first be glorified, because Pentecost is the consummation of Calvary: as in the universal sacrifice-pattern the victim is first offered and accepted (glorified) and in some way made one with deity, that then through it the divine life may come to men, so in the one Sacrifice in which mankind is redeemed, the Victim must first be offered (Calvary) and then, rising into the new life, be glorified (Ascension, ' sitteth at the right hand of God the Father '), that then the divine life may descend into the hearts of men (Pentecost). So St John had said of the ' Spirit which they should receive who believed in him,' that ' as yet the Spirit was not given, because Jesus was not yet glorified.'[3]

So the Church speaks of the Ascension as *admirabilis*: evoking wonder; and Abbot Marmion suggests why the adjective should be applied to it in particular: because it is, precisely, the summit of glory, the apotheosis. But it is still part of the redemptive process: ' he lowered his own dignity, accepted an obedience which brought him to death, death on a cross. *That is why* God has raised him to such a height, given him that name which is greater than any other

---

[1] *Spirit and Reality*, p. 125.
[2] *John*, xvi, 7.
[3] *John*, vii, 39. I have discussed this in greater detail in *The High Green Hill*, chs. VII and XIII.

name; so that everything in heaven and on earth and under the earth must bend the knee before the name of Jesus.'[1] 'That is why'; there is a strict correlation between the depths of his (redemptive) humility and the heights of his (redemptive) glory—and so the Agony-descent and the Ascension both take place in the garden of Olivet—and therefore, as St Thomas points out, the Ascension is the direct cause of our salvation, *non per modum meriti sed per modum efficientiae*, effectively causing our own ascension by 'initiating it, as it were, in our Head' (of the mystical Body of the Church) 'with whom the members must be joined.'[2]

The coming of the Spirit, then, is the direct result of the Ascension of the Son; and if we still wonder why, even so, it was 'expedient'—what it was that the Spirit could do which the Son could not—we find the answer in the very nature of the mission of the incarnate Word. All that he did was done through his human nature, for the essence of his mission is mediation, and therefore the Cross. He came too to reveal the truth; but that also he did through his humanity, teaching in the only way one man can teach another, outwardly, through the senses. But to hear the truth is not the same as to be possessed by the truth. To read the law is not the same as to have the law inscribed in the heart. After the Resurrection the Apostles, having heard the truth, remained none the less timid men, hiding behind locked doors 'for fear of the Jews'; but when 'the days of the Pentecost were accomplished' and suddenly there came the sound as of a mighty wind and the brilliance as of fire[3] and they were filled with the Holy Ghost, then they were changed men, they were inwardly transformed, they preached the wonderful works of God, not something of which they had heard, but something which had taken possession of their personalities. And it is for that inward 'possession' that the Church prays in the Whitsun liturgy:

Send forth thy Spirit and they shall be created: and thou shalt renew the face of the earth.

[1] *Phil.* ii, 8-11.
[2] *Sum. Theol.* III, lvi, 6.
[3] To be faithful to the Scripture text, an artist, depicting the scene, should give the impression of a filling of the whole room with blazing flame and power, for the greek word in the *Acts of Apostles* suggests a single sheet of flame, dividing itself into darting tongues of fire which leap at and rest over each disciple (*Acts*, ii, 3).

The Water and the Fire

Come, O holy Spirit, fill the hearts of thy faithful; and kindle in
them the fire of thy love.
Come, holy Spirit, father of the poor, light of men's hearts.
O blessed light, fill the depths of the hearts of thy faithful:
Wash away our squalors; water the arid soil; heal our wounds.

The wind and the fire are symbols of energy: to be possessed
by love is to be filled with a power which will not be denied:
which will do anything, brave anything, suffer anything, endure
anything, for the sake of what it loves. 'I can do all things in him
who strengtheneth me'; 'I am sure that neither death, nor life,
nor angels, nor principalities, nor powers, nor things present, nor
things to come, nor might, nor height, nor depth, nor any other
creature, shall be able to separate us from the love of God which
is in Christ Jesus our Lord.'[1]

So, all over the world, in the might of the Wind and the Fire
the Gospel is preached, 'in danger from rivers, in danger from
robbers . . . ; danger in cities, danger in the wilderness, danger in
the sea, danger among false brethren'[2]; all over the world the
poor and needy are succoured, the sick are nursed, the lepers are
tended, the schools and hospitals are built, the ravages of human
cruelty and folly and rapacity are repaired, the sorrowful are comforted, the desperate infused with new hope; and though again
there is darkness over the earth, still the darkness is pierced, all over
the world the fires glow, the flames leap up, so that out of the
darkness humanity can cry with St Stephen, 'I see the heavens
opened'; all over the world there are the hidden lives, the contemplatives, rapt in God, generating and radiating the redemptive
light and life and power to save the world.

There are some who think that the darkness of these present
times will in the end prove to have been creative because we
approach through it a new age, an 'age of the Spirit,' in which
the Pentecostal fire, the inner energy of love and truth, will be
more widely and manifestly operative than before. The externalization of religion into a routine observance of 'outward modes and

[1]*Phil.* iv, 13; *Romans,* viii, 38-39.
[2] *II Cor.* xi, 26.

96

forms' would then be replaced by a contrary process: a deeper and deeper internalization of doctrine and life, a flowering of the contemplative spirit, a vast outpouring of *caritas*; so that within the Church's own life the organic would more and more colour and in-form the organized, and its outward activity would be more and more fully vitalized and empowered and directed by the indwelling Spirit—the story of Pentecost realized more and more universally in the hearts of Christ's followers.

It is for the christian of today, then, to prepare himself as best he may to hasten the coming of such an age, for indeed it is easy to see the present situation as a race for time: the darkness deepens, mankind sinks lower and lower into subhumanity, and it seems clear that in so doing he becomes more and more impervious to a purely *rational* apostolate. It is said (and rightly) that we must not preach to the starving: we must give them bread. Equally we must not preach to the psychologically starving: we must bring them, we must show them, we must give them, the bread of life. For ourselves, we must have a deep understanding of the faith as a 'reasonable service': the importance of rational theology will increase rather than decrease; but unless our theological concepts are transmuted, together with the rest of the personality, in the 'crucible of fire,' it seems unlikely that any direct contact with the unbelieving world will bear much fruit. St John was a mighty theologian; but at the end he could only say again and again, 'Little children, let us love one another.' St Thomas Aquinas was a mighty theologian; but at the end all his writings seemed to him worthless. The curé d'Ars on the other hand had so little head for theology that he rarely succeeded in being priested at all, yet his penitents were numbered in thousands. For ourselves the need of theology will go on increasing; but what the world needs before it can become capable of theology is the vision behind the theology, the vision that made the *Summa Theologica* seem like straw, the vision that was distilled into St John's *Filioli*, 'Little children,' the vision that Dante embodied in a phrase of breath-taking sublimity—

> *O Luce eterna che . . . ami ed arridi—*
> 'eternal light that loves and *smiles*.'

To incarnate theology in the flesh and blood of our own lives,
our own personalities: that is the way to prepare for the age of the
Spirit, and the best (and perhaps nowadays the only) way to bring
the light and the life to those who need it.[1]

'Thou who are all fire, have mercy upon me.'

But to incarnate theology is to live in the Spirit; and to live
in the Spirit is to live the life described for us in the gifts and fruits
of the Spirit, those modes of being and acting (the poetry of the
christian life as opposed to the prose of the virtues) which are the
effect not of reasoned judgments but of the direct impulse of the
Spirit.

The septiform 'gift' establishes the fundamental attitude.[2]
We are to approach God, the *Mysterium Tremendum*, with a loving
awe which only deepens as the process of unification goes on (the
gift of fear); we are to approach him, the Father, and in degree
all lesser authorities and loyalties, and the beauty and value of all
created things, with wonder and reverence, approaching God as a
child, approaching truth as a child, approaching all reality
with the candour and sincerity of a child (the gift of
pietas); we are so to identify our own wills with the will of
God that no dangers we may encounter, no difficulties in
the work to be done, will undermine our quiet confidence that
God will empower us to overcome them (the gift of courage);
we are to look to the Spirit to make good the deficiencies of reason
in practical matters, to give us some share of that divine shrewdness, and that consequent sureness of touch, which are to be seen
in the saints and which turn the folly and failure for which men
deride them into ultimate success (the gift of counsel); we are to
develop, under the Spirit's guidance, a 'sense' of divine truth, an
ability to judge intuitively of created things *quasi oculo Dei*, as
though with the eye of God (the gift of knowledge); to penetrate
the obscurity of the secondary objects of faith—the sense of the
Scriptures, the being of the Church, the meaning of our own

[1] If, in our sloth and feebleness, we know only that we cannot in fact achieve such an
incarnation, we can but hope to achieve some measure of good by at least turning theology
into the flesh and blood of human experience, human desires, human needs; but that of
itself cannot be a substitute for the major task, nor exonerate us from the major duty.

[2] With the working of the gifts in the ordinary daily life of the christian I have attempted
to deal in greater detail in *The Divine Pity*.

nothingness before God—by the gift of understanding; and finally and supremely, though God must always remain for us here on earth the *latens deitas*, the hidden Godhead, the object not of vision but of faith, to arrive at some sort of direct experiencing of the indwelling Trinity through the life of prayer, and, through that inner union so brought about, to judge of everything *secundum altissimas causas*, in the light of ultimate reality, seeing God in all things and all things in God, as Bl. Henry Suso describes it in writing of the man who is wholly given to God: ' God has now become all things to him, and all things have become, as it were, God to him, for all things present themselves to him now in the manner in which they are in God, and yet they remain each one what it is in its natural essence '; and so elsewhere he exhorts us, ' Be steadfast, and never rest content until thou hast obtained the now of eternity as thy present possession in this life, so far as this is possible to human infirmity.'[1]

The fruits of the Spirit describe the qualities discernible in a man whose heart the Spirit has thus ' instructed.' From love, which is the source of all, the selfless, ardent love infused by the Spirit, there springs inevitably joy: a selfless joy in God which sorrows and sufferings cannot quench, for it is a sharing in that *riso de l'universo* of which Dante speaks, the laughter of the universe as it adores the Eternal Light; the joy which led Henry Suso, at the *sursum corda* of the Mass, to gather about him in spirit all creatures which God ever created, ' inciting them to sing joyously, and to offer up their hearts to God '[2]; and the love and the joy produce peace and patience, ' that inward peace which can break through all assaults and crosses of oppression, suffering, misery, humiliation and what more there may be of the like, so that a man may be joyful and patient therein, like the beloved disciples and followers of Christ '[3]; and these in their turn make a man kind and gentle, for ' his love is pure and unmixed, insomuch that he cannot but love in sincerity all men and things, and wish well, and do good to them, and rejoice in their welfare '[4]; and being patient and

[1] Suso: *Life* (1865 ed.) pp. 265
[2] *op. cit.* p. 39.
[3] *Theol. Germ.* ch. xii.
[4] *op. cit.* ch. xxxiii.

gentle he will be able to look beyond the immediate to the ultimate, to take the long view (*longanimitas*), and so, further, he will be a good and faithful servant, for he will say ' I would fain be to the Eternal Goodness, what his own hand is to a man '[1] and so will give his whole energy to doing well the work God gives him to do, and to carrying it out faithfully and doggedly to the end; and finally, if he thus lives in and for God, allowing God, as St Teresa says, to accomplish his will in him,[2] the transmutation which will thus be effected in him will restore to his personality as a whole something of that harmony and integrity which Adam knew before the Fall: the spirit will control, and operate in and through, the other levels of the personality, which will then achieve something of that *splendor formae*, that shining out of form through matter, of soul through body, which is St Thomas's definition of beauty, and the ' living flame of love ' of which St John of the Cross sings, will have achieved its purifying purpose:

> ' *O burn that searest never !*
> *O wound of deep delight !*
> *O gentle hand ! O touch of love supernal*
> *That quick'nest life for ever,*
> *Putt'st all my woes to flight,*
> *And, slaying, changest death to life eternal !*
>
> *And O, ye lamps of fire,*
> *In whose resplendent light*
> *The deepest caverns where the senses meet,*
> *Erst steep'd in darkness dire,*
> *Blaze with new glories bright*
> *And to the lov'd one give both light and heat !* ' [3]

To see the process in its fullness we have to look at the saints, whose heads are girt about with the golden beams of the Sun; but the working of the Spirit in the soul is not confined to them: it is, at least germinally, part of the stuff of every christian life, part of the effect of the initial rebirth; and the saints, so far from dis-

[1] *op. cit.* ch. x.
[2] *Exclamations of the Soul to God*, ch. vi.
[3] *Living Flame of Love*, trans. E. Allison Peers.

couraging us by the splendour of what they are and what we are so immeasurably far from being, should on the contrary give us new heart, for we live not in loneliness but in the family of the communion of saints and, like Beatrice with her *occhi ridenti*, her laughing eyes, they beckon us on and give us their prayers and their merits and their longing before God that we may be as they in the end.

For us, then, for our part to pray always:

'Thou who art all fire, have mercy upon me,'

that the dark fire, the anger-fire within us be changed into the light which is life, so that being thus transmuted in the divine creative crucible we may not only be ourselves numbered among those who dwell for ever in the light inaccessible, but may even here and now begin, in our feeble and fumbling way, to imitate those who, like the Baptist, are a 'burning and a shining light,' burning with the divine love that brings joy to the world, comfort and strengthening to the distressed and the troubled, zeal and courage to the weak and the wavering; and shining—transparent of God— so as to draw others in their turn to the 'light that enlighteneth every man that cometh into the world,' to find there the end of their wanderings, in that

luce eterna, che sola in te sidi—

the 'eternal light that alone abides within itself, alone knows itself, and, known and knowing, loves and smiles,' for it is the

Amor che muove il Sole e l'altre stelle—

the Love that moves the Sun and the other stars.'

VI

The Recovery of Symbol:
The Church's Daily Life

IN THREE ways the christian life can be called a sacramental life. First, and most important, it is sacramental inasmuch as Christ the Mediator has given to certain material things, in certain circumstances, an instrumental efficacy to be the channels of that divine life which descends from God to man. So the sacraments (the sacred signs) are said to effect, by divine disposition, what they signify. This efficacy is described by theologians as *ex opere operato*: it is not dependent on the dispositions of the recipient (apart from the possibility of a positive act—in the will—of repudiation) but is inherent in the symbol itself. As an extension of the sacramental system the Church makes use also of what are called sacramentals: other symbols, such as the use of holy water or the sign of the Cross, whose efficacy however is entirely dependent on the dispositions of the subject.

In a second sense the christian life is sacramental inasmuch as all creatures point beyond themselves, are intimations of that Infinity to whom they owe their existence and whose beauty they mirror.

Thirdly, it is not only man who is sanctified through the instrumentality of material things, but material things which are blessed by the Church as part of the process of 're-integration of all things in Christ' from that travail in which, even until now, 'every creature groaneth.'[1]

[1] *Romans*, viii, 22.

We seem to a great extent to have lost the early Church's vivid awareness of the 'new life' as affecting matter as well as spirit, body as well as soul, creation as a whole as well as humanity. For the early Fathers of the Church, as Miss Evelyn Frost has pointed out,[1] the Pauline doctrine of death as the 'wages of sin' is not to be understood exclusively of some form of spiritual death: man in sinning seems in some sense to have 'severed the flesh from direct communication with the immanent Sustainer of Life'; the new life itself, on the other hand, did include a certain liberation from the evils of the old nature, death and disease: as is shown by the 'laying on of hands' for the curing of illness through the infusion of spiritual power.[2]

But the Church's ministry of healing was not to be confined exclusively to man. The *Rituale Romanum* with its multitude of blessings still abundantly proves the contrary: blessings of houses, vehicles, bridges, springs and wells, fire, linen, barns, stables, byres, horses, cattle, birds, bees, bread, wine, all these and many others, ending with the *benedictio ad omnia*, the blessing for any thing for which there is no special formulary, all show the Church's consciousness of the fact that all the creatures involved in human existence are not only capable of but need incorporation in some sense in the 'new life.' So the *benedictio ad omnia* prays that God 'by whose word all things are sanctified' may bless the thing in question, so that whoever may use it 'according to thy will and law and with giving of thanks' may 'through the invoking of thy holy name receive from thee health of body and safety of soul.'

Perhaps we have lost sight of this because we have lost the sense of the ambivalence in things. The sun is both life-bringer and death-bringer; the sea, to recall Guardini's example, is now filled with menace, cruelty, perfidy, eternal restlessness; now gentle, healing, peaceful, the image of the infinite Sea Pacific. We forget

[1] *Christian Healing*, p. 24.
[2] The progress of medical science no doubt led to an exclusive reliance upon it for the curing of disease and to the relegation, consciously or unconsciously, of the Church's healing agency to the limbo of outmoded things, as though the two things were incompatible. It is interesting that one of the effects of modern psychological progress has been precisely to underline again the inter-relation of body and spirit, the degree to which physical disease can be psychogenic and, in consequence, the degree to which a healing of spirit may contribute to physical health.

the pervasiveness of evil: the fact that all nature is involved in the Fall of angels and of men and that therefore the maleficence must be driven out and beneficence imparted. When Christ with a word stills the wind and the waves it is not just an isolated incident but a *type*: a pre-figuring of the way in which all the time the divine regenerative power, mediated officially through the Church and individually through holy people, is meant to heal and sanctify Nature, making it an instrument in the unfolding of the story of redemption. Just as we domesticate wild animals, first taming them and then in greater or less degree incorporating them into the life of man (and the saints have sometimes domesticated the wildest of animals), so the Church first ' exorcizes ' and then blesses the water and the salt that they may become a *remedium generi humano*, an instrument for the healing of the human race.

In the Church's daily life these three aspects of sacramentalism are all vividly present if we have eyes to see: the things which are used in liturgical worship are themselves sanctified either that they may become for mankind sacraments or sacramentals, or at any rate that they may instruct the mind and the heart, and lead from the immediate finite to the Infinite.[1]

The church itself (the building) is full of such lessons and intimations. It is built above the level of the surrounding ground, so that you must mount steps to enter it: you think of the ' gradual psalms ' of the Hebrews, the pilgrims going up to Jerusalem, to Zion, to the Temple; you think of mountains (Sinai, Horeb) as the ' place of vision ' where man enters into communion with the divine, and of how among the various races and cultures of humanity mountains have been regarded as the abode of the gods. And it is a climb: it requires effort, endurance, courage: it is the ' ascent of Mt Carmel ' with all that that implies of purification and self-naughting and dedication: the house of God is not to be a den of thieves: you must leave behind you the greed and avarice, the noise and bustle of self-seeking, which deafen the spirit to the voice of God. At the Scala Santa in Rome you mount the seemingly interminable steps on your knees: so in spirit it must be with

[1] The rest of this chapter is largely an adaptation of a series of articles on the Church's symbols which appeared in *Worship* (U.S.A.) 1952-3

every church, for *terribilis est locus iste*: this place is a place of awe, the house of God and gate of heaven.

You climb the steps and enter the church in awe and humility, remembering your sinfulness, as the Mass begins with the *confiteor*, the confession of sins, and the cry for mercy of the *Kyrie*. But once inside you are to hold your head high, for there are more steps leading up to the sanctuary and more again to the altar, and it is to the altar that your eyes are drawn: to the symbol of the crucifix and to the reality of the Presence. 'I have raised my eyes to the hills,' sings the psalmist, 'whence help shall come to me'; and again, 'To thee have I raised up my eyes, who dwellest in the heavens.' Conscious of his own nothingness and his own sin, conscious of the fact that he lives in a fallen and twisted world, the christian is conscious too, and above all, of the fact that he and it are redeemed; and that from the mountain-top, from the altar, life pours down.

But the altar is as yet far from him, far away in the east where the Sun of justice rises. The Sun rises, the new dawn appears, the new life; but before man can share in it he must first go down into the darkness and the death. The neophyte must first fulfil the process described by St Paul as having been accomplished by those who share Christ's life: 'You know well enough that we who were taken up into Christ by baptism have been taken up, all of us, into his death. In our baptism we have been buried with him, died like him, that so, just as Christ was raised up by his Father's power from the dead, we too might live and move in a new kind of existence. We have to be closely fitted into the pattern of his resurrection, as we have been into the pattern of his death; we have to be sure of this, that our former nature has been crucified with him, and the living power of our guilt annihilated, so that we are the slaves of guilt no longer. . . . [You] must think of yourselves as dead to sin, and alive with a life that looks towards God, through Christ Jesus our Lord.'[1]

The neophyte then must first go down into the dark waters, into the 'laver of water to which his word gave life'[2]; and so the baptistery is built below the level of the church: he must go

---

[1] *Romans*, vi, 3-11.   [2] *Ephesians*, v. 26.

down into Christ's death, into the tomb which is also the womb, the deep waters in which pride and greed and self-idolatry are to be killed that the true self may be born. Dr Jung cites the striking example of the Holy Sepulchre of St Stefano in Bologna: 'The church itself,' he writes, 'a very old polygonal building, consists of the remains of a temple to Isis. The interior contains an artificial spelaeum [i.e. a cave where the rites of initiation were performed] a so-called Holy Sepulchre, into which one creeps through a very little door. After a long sojourn, the believer reappears reborn from this mother's womb.'[1] The waters, which themselves have first been exorcized of evil and sanctified to God's redemptive purposes, thus become the vehicle of divine power in the driving out of evil (*Exi, Satanas*) from the human being, and the entry of the holy Spirit, so that the seeds of heavenly life (*inchoatio beatitudinis*) are already within the reborn body and soul of the believer.

So the *candidatus*, the white-robed one, emerges reborn from the waters, and mounts the steps into the new life which has been given him. And all about him he finds the evidences, the characteristics, of that new life. When he enters the new life he is to leave behind him the old world of evil and greed: he does not leave behind him the earth and its fullness which are the Lord's. Whether he is in a great roman basilica or in a simple country village church he will find essentially the same things. Here are stone and wood carved into praise; here are the grape clusters and the sheaves of corn, the carved animals on choir-stall or capital, the winged lion of St Mark, the eagle of St John—and the gargoyle monsters also, to remind us that evil is still to be reckoned with; here are the arts of silversmith and weaver, and the glories of music and song; and here is the rhythm of Nature, the ' coming of the seasons, the going of the seasons.' Here the sun's rays may envelop the candidatus in gold, for he has left the darkness behind him and is a child of the light; or, caught in the magic of stained glass, the same golden glory may glitter down upon him like a thousand jewels, for this is the heavenly Jerusalem whose walls are all of precious stones and whose towers are built of gems. Here he will

[1] *Psychology of the Unconscious*, p. 209. For the already baptized christian, the confessional is similarly the darkness in which the life if lost can be regained.

find the objects proper to all the senses hallowed and turned into praise: the rhythms and colours of painting and sculpture, of hangings and vestments; the beauty of poetry and music; the smell of the upward-wreathing incense; the use of the body in gestures and movements which announce praise.

Nothing is easier, as we have seen, in a world which has lost its sense of wonder, than for such things to lose their vitality, their meaning. Words lose their magic, their evocative power and degenerate into dead labels; gestures lose their eloquence and become empty forms. But in the church, words and gestures and all the other material things are pressed into the service of the ever-living sacrifice of the altar, into the praise of the Beauty ever old and ever new; and while, if altar and sacrifice are realities to us, these things must preserve their reality too, it is also equally true that if we preserve our sense of wonder and awareness these things will continually deepen and enrich our awareness of what altar and sacrifice mean.

Just as it is not surprising, to anyone who believes in the loving and all-embracing providence of God, to find that the varied incidents of the Passion story, determined as they were by matter-of-fact contemporary events and situations, none the less embody the mythological symbolism of all humanity; so also it is not surprising to find that the details of christian worship, determined similarly by immediate practical needs and circumstances, are none the less immensely rich in symbolic significance. Thus, in the earliest days the Mass was offered in private houses and therefore on tables similar to those on which the family would take their meals; later on, in the catacombs, tombs or slabs of stone were used, and Pope St Silvester, when it became possible to build churches openly, decreed that henceforth stone must be the material on which the sacrifice was offered. But the wooden table in fact symbolizes not only the Last Supper, the sacred banquet, God's hospitality to man, but also takes us back to the wood of the Tree; the stone tomb images St Paul's doctrine of our burial with Christ that we may walk in a new condition of life; and the stone tomb and the stone slab alike symbolize the Rock which is Christ, the Corner-Stone, and take us back to the Old Testament where, just as the waters of the Red Sea are the symbol of baptism, so the manna and the water from the rock, which gave them food and drink, are prototypes of the christian supper: they drank ' the same prophetic drink, watered by the same prophetic rock which bore them company, the rock that was Christ.'[1]

Wood or tomb or rock which gives forth life-giving water: all these are symbols of rebirth, of ' newness of life.' The wood is the tree of death which is also the tree of life. (Some primitive tribes bury their dead in hollow trees, that they may live again.) The martyr's tomb in the catacomb takes the mind back to that other tomb from which Christ rose again to glorified life. The rock gives forth that water of rebirth, ' springing up into life everlasting,' of which our Lord spoke to the Samaritan woman. All three are thus mother-symbols, symbols of the womb of life: we go to our Mother (God, the Church) not in order to hide ourselves away from life but on the contrary in order that, having found renewal and freedom, we may be able to go forth again and face reality, and in the end find life in its fullness.

The same motif recurs in the white linen cloths which are spread over the altar, recalling the white clothing given to the candidatus at baptism; and again, during the Mass, in the water of the *Asperges* and the *Lavabo*. And the cross too which surmounts the altar repeats the lesson; and while the greek cross with its four equal arms is the symbol of perfection, entelechy, attainment, the latin cross, plunging down into the earth which is yet to be fully redeemed, is the symbol of the dynamic redemptive process: we are not yet at the end of the journey; the dragon is still mighty, the way is still dark. The process is yet to be completed; and we find a clue as to how it is to be completed in the candles which stand beside the cross.

Here again the origin was utilitarian: it was necessary to have lights in the catacombs. But the symbolism is immensely rich. The candle is of beeswax, the work of the ' mother bee' which the Holy Saturday liturgy celebrates and of which we read in Ecclesiasticus that, though *brevis in volatilibus*, ' an inconsiderable creature' yet ' there is a world of sweetness in the harvest she wins.'[2] The

---

[1] *I Corinth.* x, 4.   [2] *Ecclus.* xi, 3.

candle itself is upright, straight, white (*candidus* again); it gives
out both light and warmth (*candor* signifies both whiteness and
glowing heat); it consumes its life in giving praise to God. So it
gives us a sort of synopsis of the christian life. We are not to be
dismayed because we are so inconsiderable; on the contrary,
starting precisely from humility, from the sense of our own nothingness before God, we are to try to have these same qualities in ourselves and to use up our own lives creatively in praising God and
spreading about us the light of vision and the warmth of love.
Fiat lux: let there be light, let there be love: the candle flames and
glows; and when a human being gives himself to the infinite
consuming Fire the dross is indeed burnt away in him, but there
is left, not an emptiness, but the infinity of life and of love.[1]

The altar is the altar of regenerative sacrifice; and the bread
and wine which are to be used in the sacrifice are symbols of the
necessary food and drink without which life cannot be sustained;
there are also the essential fruits of the earth (God's gift) perfected
by the art of man serving the community—symbols of life therefore but as including the earth and its fullness, man and the works
of man, and the human family (which includes all that over which
man has dominion and for which he has responsibility—creation
as a whole). And the bread and wine are first manifested at the
moment of Offertory, when the priest raises them up and prays
that they may be an acceptable offering and secure for the faithful
the gift of eternal life.

St Augustine defines sacrifice in general as *oblatio rei ut sancti-
ficetur*: the offering to God of a thing in order that it may be
sanctified. The offering of a victim which is to represent the self-
offering of man is the first moment or movement of the sacrifice;
there follows, if the sacrifice is 'acceptable,' the fulfilment in the
sanctifying of the victim, the 'entering into it,' in some way, of
divine life so that again the faithful in whose place it stands may
themselves, through communicating together in it, receive that
divine life. Bread and wine, then, stand here for the human beings
offering the sacrifice in union with the Priest-Victim into whom

[1] For the symbolism of the candle cf. also *The Divine Pity*, p. 137; and of the Mass
generally, *The High Green Hill*, ch. XIII, The Sacrifice of the Mass.

the elements are soon to be changed and without whom the sacrifice could not be efficacious[1]; and they offer themselves *ut sanctificentur*, that they may be made holy through the gift of divine life. But what is included in that self-offering? It is not merely the bodies and souls of the offerers: it is their lives in the fullest sense. Life is a tissue of relationships: with other human beings, with animals and inanimate things, with the works of our own and other men's hands, with the earth and the sun and the stars. Into the cup raised by the priest in offering, therefore, we are to put ourselves, our relatives and friends, the society we live in, the whole body of the Church, the whole human family; we are to put the earth and all creatures, all human arts, occupations, joys, sorrows, that through Christ this totality may be sanctified and redeemed. (It was to this totality that Henry Suso called, at the *sursum corda*, to ' sing joyously and to offer up their hearts to God.') So, as St Augustine points out, the bread is the gathering of many grains of wheat into one loaf; the wine is formed of the juice of many grapes; and it is this unity-out-of-multiplicity that is to be offered and sanctified.

The bread is white, like the candles and the linen; the wine is red: white for the candour of truth, red for the fire of love. Behind the bread of the new dispensation there is all the Old Testament symbolism of the manna in the desert: God's care for his people; and all the human symbolism of the breaking of bread for hospitality, generosity, good fellowship. Behind this again is the universal symbolism both of the fertility rites (the ' grain of wheat,

[1]This has been put very clearly by Fr Victor White in the work already quoted. ' Something is done,' he writes, ' which we cannot do for ourselves, nor do without. The sacrifice and sacrament, to be genuine at all, must be an act of God, of which we may be the instruments or the recipients, but which we cannot originate. Paganism also has sensed that the Giver, the Gift and the Receiver of sacrifice must somehow be one, and somehow divine; . . . even in a Stone Age environment, sacrifice is considered to be a giving *of* God *by* God *to* God in and through the human priest and victim or his surrogate. St Paul sees that in the very human death on Calvary, it is " God in Christ who is reconciling the world to himself," and it is on that account that the Church dogma has insisted on the unmixed and undiluted Godhead and manhood of her Lord. It is one of the achievements of analytical psychology to have shown the psychological need to which this responds. We talk loosely of self-sacrifice, and we may mean quite heroic selflessness and altruism. But . . . that is not yet sacrifice. Self-sacrifice means whole self-giving, an unqualified renunciation of every claim on what we possess—and we do not possess ourselves. Indeed, the more we advance in self-knowledge and self-possession . . . the more we know that we are *not* our own, and therefore are incapable of self-sacrifice. Only a Lord of all, who possesses all, can initiate and consummate the sacrifice and impart to us the new life which springs from death.' (*op. cit.* pp. 230-1.)

falling into the ground '), and of the myths of the god who becomes divine food for man. Behind the wine there is a similar pagan mythology; there is also all the human story of joy and friendship; there is the gladness of human festival—but ' there is no such thing as a feast " without gods " ': to celebrate human feasts humanly is to see them as deriving from and returning to worship; while at the same time the spirit of worship induces festival: not the pessimistic, subhuman gloom of sabbatarianism, but the gladness and gaiety of Easter Sunday: ' Rejoice in the Lord always; again I say, rejoice. . . . The Lord is nigh '; a gaiety which does not despise but sanctifies the natural expressions of joy and friendship and fellowship: ' A concert of music in a banquet of wine is as a carbuncle set in gold; as a signet of an emerald in a work of gold, so is the melody of music with pleasant and moderate wine '[1]. It is significant that Albertus Magnus, writing on the Holy Eucharist, does not hesitate to apply to Christ the verse from the book of *Ruth*: ' When Booz [Christ] had eaten and drunk and was merry, he went to sleep,'[2] i.e. ' on the cross and in the tomb.'[3] Behind this again is all the deeper, divine story which is symbolized in the vineyard and the cup: ' the vineyard of the Lord of hosts is the house of Israel'; ' what is there that I ought to do more to my vineyard, that I have not done to it?' (*Isaiah*, v, 7, 4); ' I am the Lord that keep it, I will suddenly give it drink: lest any hurt come to it, I keep it night and day ' (*Isaiah*, xxvii, 3); ' thou hast prepared a table before me . . . and my chalice which inebriateth me, how goodly it is' (*Ps.* xxii, 5); ' dawn shall find us in the vineyard, looking to see what flowers the vine has, and whether they are growing into fruit . . . To my mother's house I will lead thee, my captive; there thou shalt teach me my lessons, and I will give thee spiced wine to drink ' (*Song of Songs*, vii, 12; viii, 2).

Calix inebrians, calix benedictionis: of what shape should such a cup be? In primitive and medieval times the form which predominates is what one would expect: almost stemless, with broad

---

[1] *Ecclus.* xxxii, 7-8.
[2] *Ruth*, iii, 7.
[3] ' It is characteristic of the great-hearted (*magnifici*),' he writes, *delectari et hilarescere* ' in *magna donando*: ' to delight and be merry in the giving of great gifts'; and he quotes the verse of *Proverbs* (xix, 12) that the hilarity of a king is ' as the dew upon the grass.' (*De Eucharistia*, ii, 1.)

base and very wide and rather shallow cup: for the cup should indeed be wide, wide enough to receive the infinite prodigality of God and to elicit an answering generosity from man. In later times, the Renaissance and after, the shape alters to long ornate stem and narrow tulip-shaped cup. It is tempting to see behind this change a loss of charity, a wordliness, and a sort of jansenist narrowing-down of God's universal love; it is certainly heartening to notice the widespread return in these days to the older design.

During the offering of the Mass and throughout its daily worship the Church tries to make contemplatives of us, not only by teaching us how to turn our minds and hearts to prayer, but also by showing us how to turn our bodies into prayer—if only we do not allow custom to turn what should be a vital creative process into an empty routine.

As the christian enters the church he takes holy water and makes the sign of the Cross. The water is primarily a re-enactment of baptism: it has particular reference to the driving out of Satan, to exorcism, and the vanquishing of evil within us, the putting aside of all that we mean by 'the spirit of the world,' of worldliness, as we enter the temple of God. And the sign of the Cross recalls first of all the Sacrifice for the offering of which the church is built, but also gathers together the whole personality—the four points of the compass—in strength and inwardness: distractions, super-ficialities, all the things that lead us away from God, the 'little foxes, thieving among the vineyards' of which the *Song of Songs* speaks, all these are to be put away that the whole personality may be turned wholly to God.

There follows the genuflection to the altar; which is to set the whole psychological atmosphere for what follows. In itself an act of homage, like a feudal act of obeisance to the liege lord,[1] it is at the same time a symbolic representation of an attitude of mind and heart: before God we are nothingness, created by him *ex nihilo*, ourselves the 'first cause' only of evil, as St Thomas points out; and in addition we are separated from him by the abyss of evil within us. We come indeed to give praise to God; but before we can praise we must confess the nothingness and the evil and beg

---

[1] Cf. *His Will is our Peace*, ch. II, pp. 19-21.

God's mercy. So, in the Mass, the priest comes to the *Gloria in excelsis* and raises his arms high in a gesture of adoring praise as he intones it, only when first he has bowed low at the *Confiteor*, striking his breast, and then, with hands joined in supplication, recited the repeated *Kyrie eleison*. And yet in the sorrow itself there is joy, the joy of redemption: there is nothing here of the Uriah Heep: the Roman Mass opens with the proud cry from the psalmist: 'I will go up to the altar of God, the God who rejoices my youth'—and we may take the words, not necessarily as referring to physical youth, but as meaning that God rejoices, and by rejoicing preserves in us, our youthfulness of heart, those qualities of the *puer aeternus* we considered in an earlier chapter. Similarly the christian entering the church turns his eyes proudly to the tabernacle 'whence help comes' to him; and yet at the same time expresses in the words and gestures of humility and contrition the fact that the condition of all sacrifice is humility, as we are taught indeed in the words of the offertory prayer: 'In the spirit of humility and with a contrite heart receive us, O Lord.' St John Chrysostom, in a glorious phrase, tells us: *Ut leones ignem spirantes, ita a mensa secedimus illa*: 'it is as lions breathing fire' that we must go down from the table of the sacrifice-banquet; but the degree to which we are thus filled with divine fire will be dependent on the degree of intensity with which, before and during and after the sacrifice, we can say the prayer,

'Thou who art all fire, have mercy upon me.'

The hands are to be joined in prayer: it is again a symbol of the gathering of the personality, of strength and concentration. Men will sometimes join the tips of the fingers when engaged in concentrated thought or exposition; but here it is the entire hands which are closely joined, a concentration not merely mental but personal, a gathering of all the powers in a total act of worship.[1]

[1] As an extension of the liturgical principle of the use of the body in prayer it is interesting to recall the various ways in which St Dominic habitually prayed: (a) bowing down before the altar, and praying 'Lord, I am not worthy'; (b) lying prone on the ground and praying 'Lord, be merciful to me a sinner'; 'My soul hath cleaved to the ground: quicken thou me according to thy word'; (c) genuflecting again and again, and praying 'Lord, if thou wilt thou canst make me clean'; (d) standing erect, sometimes with hands outstretched before his breast as if reading a book before God, sometimes using the gesture of the priest reading the prayers at Mass; (e) stretching out his arms in the form of a cross and praying, 'O Lord, I have stretched out my hands to thee'; (f) erect like an arrow pointing to heaven,

'The eyes of the saint make all beauty holy,' writes Fr Thomas Merton, 'and the hands of the saint consecrate everything they touch to the glory of God.'[1] It is because the eyes of the saint are 'always on the Lord,' and the hands of the saint are concerned always to bless. In the eyes of Beatrice, Dante saw not his own reflection but that of Christ; but we for our part know all too well how our eyes mirror not God but our own pride and lust and avarice and meanness, and how often our hands are used not for blessing but for greed and cruelty and violence and self-assertion. It is to counteract all this that the Church teaches us to join our hands in prayer and adoration; to hold them out before us, the palms upward in the immemorial attitude of supplication and acknowledgement of lordship, as we take the paten and receive the Communion; and to handle with quiet reverence all the material things which are used in the liturgy, so that we may in the end become not proud and predatory but gentle. Then, instead of deepening the curse which rests on Nature as the result of original sin, we shall instead impart a blessing.

The power of blessing bestowed by God in the Old Testament on kings and priests and fathers of families—a blessing often given by the imposition of hands on the head—descends in the New Dispensation primarily to bishops and priests, in bowing before whose blessings, as Caesarius of Arles expressed it, the faithful receive a grace *per hominem, non tamen ab homine*: given through man but not by man, for it is God who blesses through the instrumentality of those who represent him.

The power of blessing is given primarily for the sake of human beings: primarily, but, as we have seen, far from exclusively. And the blessings in the *Rituale* are blessings proper to the *ecclesia docens*; but in a secondary and analogous sense every christian, sharing as he does in the priesthood of Christ, is meant to share also in the

[1] *Seeds of Contemplation*, ch. I.

with arms joined above his head, or else opened as though to receive something from heaven; (g) after the liturgical offices or the readings in the refectory: sitting quietly in his place, reading and kissing the book and bowing his head, praying 'I will hear what the Lord shall speak in me'; (h) on his journeys (which he made on foot) he would say the verse from *Osee*: 'I will lead [Israel] into the wilderness [solitude] and I will speak to her heart.' (Cf. *Analecta Ordinis Prædicatorum*, 1922.) On his journeys St Dominic would also frequently sing his worship to God.

blessing of the world and all creatures: his hands also are meant to 'consecrate everything they touch to the glory of God.'

And to the degree in which he allows the Church to form him, body and soul, into a truly christian personality this will inevitably be so. The animal-lover, who tames and domesticates and gives 'new life' to animals, making them once again part of the human family; the artist and the craftsman treating their materials with love and reverence and understanding them through their sense of touch, and so turning them into things of beauty; the farmer, who knows and loves the soil and the seasons and the ways of the earth; the poet, for whom words are things in themselves and not just labels; the gardener who brings forth order and colour and gaiety from the ground: all these and many more are sharing in the work of re-creating in some degree the un-fallen age, the state of things when man's world was a garden and he exercised a loving dominion over the creatures that God had made. And when they do this as part of their love of God and their sharing in Christ's redemptive work, then indeed they are sharing also in the Church's work of benediction, as when Bl Jordan of Saxony, having commanded the ermine to come out of its hiding-place in the hedge and show its white coat to his novices, then blessed it and bade it go back and praise God; they are themselves turning their work into praise and worship, and for that very reason their work is filled with power for the renewal of the face of the earth.

At the same time they are also fulfilling the injunction with which the Mass ends: *Ite, missa est*, Go, the Mass is ended and now the day's redemptive life must begin in the world. The christian must climb the steps to the church, and again to the sanctuary where the sacrifice is offered and the divine life given; but it is not in order that he may remain upon the mountain-top of vision: there is redemptive work to be done in the everyday world. The *Ite, missa est* is a command to descend again into the plains: for himself, he must be, like the candle, a 'being of praise,' but also he must be like the candle in the Gospel that is not to be hid under a bushel: he must go back into the world bearing with him the redemptive Christ; and, in the power of Christ, must, again like the candle, spread about him in the world the candour of truth and the glowing heat of divine love, precisely because he bears within him that ' light for the revelation of the peoples ' in whose power and whose presence there is peace and tranquillity and benison for mankind and for the earth.

VII

The Recovery of Love

JUST AS sex without love is spiritually sterile, so life without love is sterile. It is love of beauty apprehended that impels the artist to express his vision; it is love of human beings in need that sends the missionary into distant and dangerous lands or into 'God's underground'; the love of knowledge fires the scientist, of wisdom the philosopher, of God the mystic, of adventure and discovery the explorer, of the beauty of movement the dancer, of the beauty of sound the musician. It is the love of making that drives every man to be in some way creative.

Are we to conclude then that an age like our own, which has become so largely uncreative, must have lost to a great extent the meaning of love? There is perhaps a clue in this fact : that the simplest way to understand man's love of God and its growth to perfection, is to understand the love of human beings for each other and its growth to perfection; yet what the mystics tell us of the first may easily frighten us and persuade us that this is a path too difficult to follow; and if we do not reach the same conclusion with regard to human love is it because when we say we love we mean in fact something quite different?

In essentials the paths of the two loves follow an identical pattern. This is made very clear in a passage from M. Gustave Thibon's wise book, *What God has Joined Together*, where many of the ideas we have been considering in the last chapters re-appear, often clothed in strikingly similar phraseology.

He is writing of the 'transfiguring of love,' as the mystics write of the 'transmutation of the personality'; and he points out that human love, like the love of God, has its dark 'nights,' the dryness which 'when surmounted leads to the transfiguring of love, when accepted meanly and selfishly brings love to the grave.[1]

'Intimacy,' he goes on, ' is the great test of love. . . . The slow discovery of the *reality* of the loved being destroys little by little the inner idol of the loved one, the idol that was none other than the *idealized projection of the self*, the image of what the lover himself lacked. The discovery of *the other* is a bitter experience for narcissist idolatry . . .'[2] (This could describe also the beginnings of what some spiritual writers have called the 'second conversion': the shattering of what had hitherto passed for religion in men's minds, the worship of an idol, a projection, the God they had fashioned in their own image, the protective Mother in whose lap they could be comforted and petted and could hide from reality. But when all this is brought crashing down about their ears, then, if they are not 'mean and selfish' but humble and great-hearted they may meet Reality at long last, and being at long last ' stripped and poor and naked ' may begin to know God ' as he is.')

This moment of discovery of *the other*, continues M. Thibon, ' is the moment for heroism, for a holy war . . . it is the moment for *believing* in the loved one, in spite of disillusionment, in spite of the rapture that is dead; it is the moment that proclaims to lovers, whatever the illusions and baser elements in their love: Even now there is time to save from perishing that germ of eternity in your love when it was new.' (So the mystics have made great use of a verse from *Job* which, according to one reading, says: ' Even though he slay me, yet will I trust him '; and the roman breviary uses for the office of many of the saints an adaptation of a phrase of St Paul's in *Philippians* (iii, 8): ' The kingdom of this world and all the beauty of life I have esteemed as nothing, compared with the high privilege of knowing Christ Jesus my Lord,' and continues: *quem vidi, quem amavi, in quem credidi, quem dilexi*: ' for I caught sight of him and fell in love with him,' and then

---

[1] *op. cit.* p. 127.

[2] ' He worships a woman. You think such idolatry deserves to be punished? No need to worry. His idol will see to that, in a way that will more than satisfy your indignation— or even your malice! ' (Thibon, *op. cit.* p 158.)

when the darkness had fallen again upon my soul I none the less 'trusted in him,' and so in the end came to 'love him' with that deep, deliberate, enduring love which nothing can destroy. *Amo* and *diligo* both mean to love, but the first may indeed include 'illusions and baser elements': it is the *credidi* which purifies the soul of the dross and saves the 'germ of eternity' and causes it to spring up into bud and flower and fruit.)

'Whoever continues to love in spite of disillusionment,' M. Thibon goes on, 'succeeds at last in loving the object for itself. There then occurs a kind of reversal of feeling: to the gross subjectivity of first love there succeeds a complete loss of self.' (The essential 'self-naughting' of the mystical process.) 'The lover learns the reality of love; he feels himself bound to the other, overcome by the other, overpowered by a strange destiny.' (The discovery of the All: the spark returning to the Fire, the iron burned incandescent in the Fire; St Paul's 'I know that neither . . . death nor life . . . shall separate us from the love of God.') 'And he experiences a new joy: the solemn joy of self-surrender, silent and imperishable.' (St Paul's joy which is the fruit of the Spirit, the joy of selfless adoration and wonder, which no pain or sorrow can destroy.) 'Moreover, what he loves now is the very poverty of the beloved. The poorer the creature the more he has to give.' (If we love God it is because he is lovable; but God loves us in order to make us lovable. 'The poorer the creature the more he has to give.' And yet there is some corresponding mystery in God's love of man which some of the mystics have sensed and have struggled to express; as when Angelus Silesius writes of the poverty of God, or Eckhart of God's *need* of man's love, or the Lady Julian of Norwich of the 'love-longing' of Christ.[1] The fine flower of love is tenderness; but it is difficult to be tender if you can find in the beloved no poverty, no weakness, no failings. Was it partly

---

[1] 'God *needs* man,' said Eckhart; and quoting the words of Christ, 'I stand at the door and knock and wait,' goes on: 'thou needst not seek him here or there; he is no farther off than the door of the heart . . . to wait until thou openest is harder for him than for thee. He needs thee a thousand times more than thou canst need him.' (*Pred. iii*, quoted Underhill, *Mysticism*, p. 133.)

And the Lady Julian writes: 'For as verily as there is a property in God of ruth and pity, so verily there is a property in God of thirst and longing. . . . This is his thirst and love-longing, to have us altogether whole in him, to his bliss.' (*Revelations of Divine Love*, the 13th Revelation, ch. xxxi.)

for this that the Incarnate was made indigent and needy and bereft of love?)

'His love,' continues M. Thibon, 'is now chaste and tender: he would offer himself wholly to the loved one without making the smallest demand in return. It is something far higher than mere exchange, than the *do ut des*; it even thrives on disillusion-ment.' (So William Law writes that 'love has no by-ends,' as St Paul had written that 'charity seeketh not her own': and having no by-ends, being wholly disinterested, it only thrives on ingratitude.)

'But it is true here also that he who is willing to lose his life will receive it back again immortal. He who has given all is in a condition to receive all. Loved in so disinterested a way, the creature is an inexhaustible source of delight. In the hour of dryness the lover believed he had touched the bedrock of his love, but all he had reached was the bedrock of his desire, the bedrock of his idol. But idols are not deep. Now, for the first time, he discovers the soul of the beloved. . . . For it is only to hearts free from con-cupiscence that creatures ever reveal their authentic treasures; they never offer what is deep and eternal in their being except to him who has loved them first for everything they lacked.' (The mystics' poverty of spirit, 'having nothing yet possessing all things.')

'Pleasure-love and vanity-love are now left behind. Man is no longer the tortured slave of his desire; he is the slave of a soul, and in such dependence finds peace and freedom. It is unspeakably serene, this affection that rises out of the void: it knows nothing of fears or doubts or jealousies.' (The fruits of the Spirit are joy, peace, faithfulness . . .) The soul at last understands the true nature of love, defined of old as a " going out from oneself" (*amor trahit amantem extra se*), the "wishing well" to another soul.' (So the pseudo-Denys said that 'divine love causes ecstasy, i.e. a going out from oneself; and that God himself suffered ecstasy on account of love'; and St Thomas explains how the same is true of human love; it is the mystics' being 'purely, simply, and wholly at one with the One Eternal Will of God.')

'What is most important of all, at this crisis of love, is to know how to die in order to be born again. There must be no resisting the transformation effected by the trial. . . . In the hours of dryness the most dangerous temptation to lovers is that of returning to the cradle of their affection. " Remember," said the troubadour, " how our love began." But . . . the joy that the trial engenders is not the same as that which was lost; it is *another* joy. . . . Our tomorrows must never be botched-up yesterdays, they must be yesterdays transfigured.' (Unless the grain of wheat . . . But deep down inside us there is the longing to escape the ardours and perils of the dark journey: the longing to return to the ' cradle,' the womb, the ' longing for quiet and for the profound peace of non-existence, for a dreamless sleep in the ebb and flow of the sea of life' of which Jung speaks. But ' if, like Peirithoos, [man] tarries too long in this place of rest and peace, he is overcome by torpidity, and the poison of the serpent paralyzes him for all time. If he is to live he must fight and sacrifice his longing for the past, in order to rise to his own heights.'[1])

' The voyage of Columbus to America is a wonderful symbol of the transforming effects of love. First he turns his back on the east, on all the cradles of the dawn; without looking back he plunges into the realm of night, leaving behind all the things of childhood, only to find, at the farthest confines of the western ocean, an eternal orient, an unchanging dawn—and the *Pacific* Ocean. For if joy was the companion of love at its birth, *peace in joy* is to be found only after a painful pilgrimage.'[2]

Let us then repeat the question: if we are not afraid of human love as we are afraid of divine love, is it because when we say love we mean something quite different? Is it because (to use Prof. Martin Buber's language), when we say *I-Thou* we mean in fact *I-It*?

' The primary word *I-Thou* can only be spoken with the whole being.

' The primary word *I-It* can never be spoken with the whole being . . .

' All real living is meeting . . .

' If I face a human being as my *Thou*, and say the primary

[1] *Psychology of the Unconscious*, p. 215.
[2] G. Thibon: *op. cit.* pp. 127-132.

word *I-Thou* to him, he is not a thing among things, and does not consist of things . . . nor he is a nature able to be experienced and described, a loose bundle of named qualities. But with no neighbour, and whole in himself, he is *Thou* and fills the heavens. This does not mean that nothing exists except himself. But all else lives in *his* light.

' To man the world is twofold, in accordance with his twofold attitude. He perceives what exists round about him—simply things, and beings as things. . . . On the other hand, man meets what exists and becomes as what is over against him, always simply a *single* being and each thing simply as being. . . . The world which appears to you in this way . . . cannot be surveyed, and if you wish to make it capable of survey you lose it. . . . It is not outside you, it stirs in the depths of you; if you say " Soul of my soul " you have not said too much. But guard against wishing to remove it into your soul—for then you annihilate it.'[1]

' Guard against wishing to remove it into your soul '—but that is just what the possessive man wants to do. Guard against wishing simply to ' experience ' it—but that is just what the hedonist wants to do. Guard against idolizing it—but that is what the narcissist does with his ideal projection. And none of these things is love, In the christian liturgy the man is to say to the woman, With my body I thee worship—but does he in fact say I-Thou, or I-It? There is a sort of love that passes muster to experience and experiment with, to play with, to describe and survey, to utilize, to dominate with, but it can never be the love that is ' spoken with the whole being.' There is nothing creative there, because there is nothing which has gone, or will ever go, through the creative darkness.

We are many-levelled beings; and the love which is ' spoken with the whole being ' includes all the levels—and the darkness too must include them all.

The love of two people for each other is seldom if ever equal; and this inequality can itself be a darkness unless it is creatively faced and met. The two sexes differ, at every level; more than that, every individual is unique, a mystery; and on account of these

[1] M. Buber: *I and Thou*, pp. 3, 11, 8, 32-3.

things too there will be darkness. Within any individual there are all the possibilities of tension between the different levels: there is the tendency of passion to assert its own autonomy. And finally, though there may be the 'germ of eternity' in any love, there may all too easily be other elements—the 'pleasure-love and vanity-love,' the greed, the possessiveness, the unreality. It is not easy out of all these things to make a union which is real and deep and personal. It must at best be a long process; and it must include darkness. After the *vidi* and *amavi* there will have to be the *credidi* before the perfect love is achieved.

It must be a long, and often dark and arduous, process on the level of physical passion, if the passion is to be really an expression of—and a creation of—love, and not just a seeking after isolated pleasure. If it is to be both a shared joy, desired by both, and a shared voyage of discovery, longed for by both, there will be a constant need of adjustment and of self-sacrifice to accord with the temperamental differences and the constantly differing demands and possibilities of the moment. 'With my body I thee worship': not 'My body worships thy body'—the isolated pleasure-seeking; not 'I worship thee'—the ideal-projection, the fantasy figure; not 'With my body I seize thee, I subjugate thee, I possess thee'—the lust for power that can be stronger even than the lust for lust; but 'With my body I worship thee': I approach thee with wonder and awe and tenderness and humility, for 'Thou' is a mystery, and love is a mystery, and human sex is a mystery, and the body is a mystery; and so they all have to be learnt slowly, gradually, lovingly, patiently, humbly, like a poem or a symphony; and it is *thee* I worship with my body, the real person, this human being with these faults and weaknesses, these poverties and needs; and so here, and there, and again I will try to say 'Not my will but thy will be done'; and so, out of the darkness the discovery will come. Marriage 'will never be given new life except by that out of which true marriage always arises, the revealing by two people of the *Thou* to one another.'[1]

If it is difficult for two to be really and deeply one on the level of physical passion, what are we to say of the level of mind? For

---

[1] Buber, *op. cit.* pp. 45-6.

here again, as we shall see more in detail later, the two sexes differ profoundly: in so far as one can talk of ' types ' of mind, the minds of man and woman are typically different, and for that very reason are complementary, but at the price of what efforts of mutual understanding![1] And again there are beyond these general differences the individual differences, the ways of thought of *this* particular individual and *that* one. There will be tensions, misunderstandings, blindnesses, impatiences; there will be no lack of ' dark nights ' here.

And beneath all this again, the struggle for union between the two wills: the need of constant adjustment in the clash of small immediate wants and reluctances, likes and dislikes; the constant effort to create together a deep underlying unity of purpose; and the ' holy war ' to surmount triumphantly the inequalities of love without which to be loved too little causes the aridity of frustration and to be loved too much produces the aridity of satiety and impatience.

So we return to the needs of love from which human beings so easily shy away in fear: the discovery of reality, the poverty of spirit, the acceptance of darkness, the ' ecstasy,' the self-naughting, the determination to leave all the ' cradles of the dawn ' and plunge ' into the realm of night,' so as to find in the end the ' eternal orient,' the Pacific Ocean.

And how is it to be done? ' As soon as we love,' writes Prof. Guitton, ' we become aware that love demands a setting in which we can love one another. We can only love truly if we love in a sphere which is superior to us, in a unity more lofty and more fulfilled, in a plenary term which assures the union of the other two. Just as respiration supposes an atmosphere, so love calls for an *erosphere*. For those who have no religion at their disposal, this common term will be simply the personification of love; they will say that they love in their love. '' Do that for the sake of our love.'' For others, the *erosphere* will be a common ideal: country, science. . . . But the true and real term which unites the loves, which estab-

---

[1] As Dr Jung notes, ' The elementary fact, that a man always presupposes another's psychology as being identical with his own, aggravates the difficulty [of mutual comprehension between the two types of psyche] and hinders a correct understanding of the feminine psyche.' (*Contributions*, p. 168.)

lishes them, without which they can neither understand each other nor expand, is that which men have named God. In fact the third term should be a being which is present in the two other beings, assuring their interchange in spite of space and time; it can only be so if it is itself superior to time, to space, and is itself capable of love, let us even say, wholly defined by love. That is why, even for the unbeliever, love (if it is total) necessarily becomes religious; it passes beyond the mutual ecstasy with which it begins and rises to an unique adoration.'[1]

We may have fought shy of the darkness which lies in the way to God, and have thought to find refuge in the human love to which we gave another definition more suited to our own comfort, a constant tarrying in the ' cradles of dawn,' in the protective womb ; but if once we discover our mistake (and unless we do we are lost: the ' poison of the serpent ' will paralyze us for all time) we discover also that, so far from having escaped the dark journey, we are thrown doubly into it. There is no discovering the reality of human love without it; but equally there is no discovering the real depth and perfection of human love unless the discovery is a shared voyage of discovery of God—and we find ourselves thrown, not only into the darkness of the human journey, but into the deeper darkness of the divine.

Yet this should not dismay us further: on the contrary, it should give us new heart. To seek God alone in the darkness might well be a terrifying thing; to embark on the journey hand in hand with one you love is to rob the journey of many at least of its terrors. We need only recall the *Paradiso*: first there is the *Guardami ben*: ' Look well, I am, I am indeed Beatrice '—and ' a thousand longings . . . fixed his eyes upon her radiant eyes'; but when he gazes into them it is Christ he sees, like the sun reflected in a glass; and when she tells him, *Al carro tieni or gli occhi*, ' Fix now your eyes upon the chariot,' he does not find it hard to obey her.[2]

' It is not good for man to be alone.' The christian sacrament

---

[1] Jean Guitton: *Essay on Human Love*, pp. 82-3.

[2] To say that such a way to God is easier is not to say that it is simpler. There will be difficulties to overcome which do not confront the man who ' goes out from all things ' and has no other thought but the God he is seeking. There will be tensions between the

of marriage has as its negative purpose to empower human beings to combat and surmount the many dangers which beset love and which, without that power, might well be expected to destroy it. But there is the positive purpose also, and it is twofold, and this shared discovery of God is the first part of it. The love of the two for each other is meant itself to help them in the finding of their erosphere; to enable them to find that which their love needs and points to; so that what, alone, they might have lacked the courage or energy to achieve, together they are to find themselves impelled to achieve, and to achieve with joy.

The second thing follows. They will not only come to find and understand and love God and his love: they will come to imitate his love. As we have seen, we love things because they are lovable: with God it is the other way round: things become lovable because he loves them. And this, human love can imitate. As life goes on, the two can perfect each other through their love: can bring to perfection the qualities proper to each. The man can, through his tender, humble cherishing of her, lead the woman to grow in depth and strength and in her own feminine tenderness; the woman can, through her love and loyalty and absorption in his vocation, lead the man to the perfection of his male qualities: his power and strength purged of brutality and aggressiveness, his ambition purged of ruthlessness, his protectiveness purged of condescension, his concern with the immediate purged of impatience and shortsightedness. And each can teach the other to be deeper, wiser, more human and so in the end more divine.

But the greatest single human factor in this process of finding their own unity, and finding God, and imitating God, will no doubt be their common creation, out of their union of two in one and as 'ministers of God's omnipotence', of the third thing, the child, which is the expression of their love. Here too they will be imitating God, they will be imitating the creative Word; but they will also be imitating the Word made flesh, who went down into darkness and death. In the beginning indeed there may be nothing

---

human love and the divine; temptations to forget the latter for the sake of the former. St Paul makes this clear enough (*I Cor.* vii, 32-4). But against all that, given the *will*-to-achieve, there will be the constant help and support, the mutual strengthening, the sustaining arms. . . .

but the joy and song of the first Christmas. A deliberately childless marriage (deliberate, that is to say, in the sense that a child would be an intruder into a self-sufficient love, a closed circle) is of its nature a frustrated thing, sterile and therefore self-destructive; for love of its nature is creative. But at the same time, procreation from a sort of cold-blooded sense of duty would equally be a monstrosity. Prof. Guitton is here very wise. Plotinus, he writes, ' said that action is a product and a weakened image of contemplation, that he who contemplates should not will the result of his contemplation, that this result proceeds naturally from the act of contemplating. A dancer thinks of nothing and yet his footsteps make patterns on the ground. It is in this sense that generation is not the *end* of love, but its result, its irradiation, its echo and its image. When there are two there are three; or rather, when the two become only one, a third term is born.'[1]

The child, then, is joy; but procreation does not end with the birth of the child or with the passing of its infancy: it does not end until the child becomes man, and leaves his home to embark on his own journey. And before that there will again be much darkness: for this indeed is a school of unselfishness. It may be that the child must be lost in order to be found; it will certainly come about that in one way or another he will cause much ' anguish of mind ' to his parents; perhaps he will have to undergo an agony and a passion which his parents will have to share with him. Yet such darknesses as these are creative. The parents' love of each other creates the child; but also the making of the child makes perfect their love.

The child is the ' extension ' of the personalities and of the lives of the parents; but there is another such extension, as we have seen, necessary to parents and child alike: the home. For just as a work of art needs its predestined setting, so that if you put an altar-piece into a museum something dies in it; so love needs its setting, the personality needs its complement, its home, and if the home is destroyed or taken away something in the love and in the personality dies.

Today the settled home with its plot of land, great or small,

[1] Guitton: *op. cit.* p. 82.

which has been handed down from generation to generation, is becoming increasingly rarer. The 'great' families are forced to leave by economic pressure, and with their going something organic in the local community dies: the sense of a family grouped round the great house and dependent in many ways on its leadership and sense of responsibility—a thing which you still find for instance as late as Fielding—is yet further lost: society becomes a *corpus acephalum*, a headless trunk, more and more amorphous, less and less a community, and must look for its leadership, not to a local squire who knew his district and its needs, but to remote and nameless bureaucrats who know neither. The small families break up in their turn; the young drift away from the country to the towns; the process of disintegration is carried further. Stability, rootedness, sense of tradition, are necessarily lost. There are many too who, through no desire of their own but by force of circumstances (from the accepted demands of work or career to the horrors of forced migration and political exile) are compelled to move from place to place. Is there any way in which a family so uprooted and perhaps condemned to perpetual wandering can have a home?[1]

The answer would seem to be, Yes, in essentials; though it is admittedly a question of making the best of a bad job. A home is primarily not a thing of bricks and mortar but of the spirit: the spirit created by the common life of the personalities concerned, and the impress of those personalities on their material surroundings. The *lares* and *penates* of modern man may be some few cherished possessions which, when everything else is left behind, are never left behind but form the nucleus of the new environment; they may on the other hand be simply the power of human personalities

[1] 'You cannot,' of course, 'put the clock back.' No; but neither is it a good thing to stop the clock altogether. That the structure of society should undergo constant development and change is a sign of vitality: provided that the change is really a development. But it will not be a development unless, whatever the changes, the organic remains organic. If you kill the organism and substitute an organization, that is not development but death: you stop the clock. And as effective power in modern society becomes more and more centralized, remote and impersonal, society itself becomes more and more organized, less and less organic. That wealth and power should not be concentrated in the hands of a few, while the many lack reasonable security and independence, has been a commonplace in papal teaching since *Rerum Novarum*; but concern for social justice has always gone hand in hand, in that teaching, with a true appreciation of the meaning of human community. The sort of social theory which sets out to remedy unjust inequalities of wealth and power while at the same time destroying the human-ness of society, is doing, in the long run and whatever its intentions, immeasurably more harm than good.

to impress themselves, their spirit, on entirely new surroundings, and in that way to give the new dwelling-place the same ' feel,' the same family atmosphere, as the old.

What is certain is that, just as God does not simply create the world once and for all and then leave it to its devices, but constantly creates it, ' conserves it in being ' all the time; so also a home is something that has to be constantly, daily, created or rather con-created by the efforts of all the members of the family in their different ways. And that too means constant self-sacrifice, constant poverty of spirit, constant self-naughting. The individuals are ' made ' in part by their home life; but equally the home is made by the individuals if they are unselfish enough to subordinate what they want to what the family needs. None the less there will be plenty of tensions between not merely the desires but the needs of individuals and the needs of the whole: once again there is plenty of room for ' darkness ' here.

Because the home is the extension of personalities and contributes to the making of personalities, it is the catholic doctrine that property is man's natural right. A social system, whatever it may call itself, which robs human beings of this right to own their own home and plot of land is destroying humanity, whether it does so with brutal tyranny or with mild benevolence. A system which robs men of their little bit of property robs them of their independence, their initiative, their pride in the good sense of the word; and though it lull them with unlimited ' bread and circuses ' the damage remains the same: it is still the evil mother, the death-mother, lulling her children into ' immobility, satiety and rest ' till they are ' overcome by torpidity ' and the ' poison of the serpent ' paralyzes them for all time. It lulls them into the false security of a world of unreality; and when humanity is thus forced into unreality, and debarred from escape into reality, it will look for escape in yet further unreality: in physical or mental drugs, in neuroses, in fantasy-worlds of its own making which ape the world it has lost as the devil is the ape of God. It will look for escape in destruction, perhaps self-destruction, as a substitute for the creativeness it has lost. The restlessness of the night-club replaces the tranquillity of the home; the restlessness of loveless sexuality replaces the stability of marriage; toys of one sort or another replace the children who should have played with them; hooliganism and thuggery, murder and suicide, the will-to-destroy and the will-to-death, replace the frustrated creative energy and zest for life.

A man's home is his castle, fulfilling his natural right to his own property, his own hearth, and his need of security and the unity of the family. A man's home is his castle: it must not become his prison. It may be his temptation to make it so: to refuse the challenge of life, and to sink, within its comforts, into torpidity; it may be the woman's temptation to make it so for him: to keep him by her when he should be adventuring forth—and so she betrays her vocation by failing to help him to the fulfilment of his. A man's home is his castle: but it must not be a closed circle or it will die of inanition: the door is there and must be used, the door that leads outwards to adventure and inwards to the hospitable hearth which receives the stranger and the wayfarer. For those within, love must have its erosphere: ' Where there is no God there is no man,' said Berdyaev; ' that is what we have learnt from experience '; love, therefore, must seek its happiness, its fulfilment, in poverty of spirit; must make its joy part of a greater joy-in-God; must make its own perfecting a fruit of the shared seeking for God, the shared love of God's will. And when it does that, then indeed the doors are open and the hearth glows for the guest: for the home will then be essentially the spirit of divine love, the love that goes out into the highways and hedges and compels them to come in that the Lord's table may be filled; and it is then that love fulfils its essential nature, creative and re-creative, and that the darkness, whatever form it may have taken, is transformed into light.

There is a very practical point to which all this leads us. The darkness which is part of the creative process of human love may be simple or complex, may be a question of small setbacks or of high tragedy: but whether it be the material out of which great poetry is made or be so drab and perhaps ridiculous as not to bear recounting, in either case the facing of it must be something severely matter-of-fact, must be a question of practical, matter-of-fact acts of will: I will or I will not, I understand and sympathize or I have no patience, I will say the word *I-Thou* or I will say the word *I-It*; and if the facing of the problems is creative it matters little in the end whether the problems themselves are high tragedy or something more like low comedy: the result can be the same.

The same is true of the search for God. If, when we read of the exalted and often terrifying lives of the great mystics, we decide (in what is perhaps an all too transparent process of rationalization) that anything so uncomfortable is not for us, and murmur to ourselves the words of the psalmist, *neque in mirabilibus super me*: ' Lord, I am not haughty of heart, nor are my eyes arrogant, neither have I moved among great matters, and things too arduous for my strength '—if we do that, we deceive ourselves. The ecstasies are not for us, nor the glories and anguish of the highest mystical states, no; we shall not be with St Francis in his stigmata or St John of the Cross in his Calvary; nor on the other hand shall we expect to know the intimacy of St Catherine of Siena's colloquies with the divine wisdom, or share in the divine familiarity of some of St Teresa's remarks to her Lord. There are other ways to the same end: the perfect love of God has many modes.

We might learn, for instance, from the simplicities of the seventeenth-century Carmelite lay-brother, Bro Lawrence, whose life in the community kitchen was so unlike that of the more spectacular of the saints that it was said of him in the contemporary preface to his little *Conversations* and *Letters* that his ' saintliness is only fully seen now that he is dead.'

' Having found in many books,' he writes, ' different methods prescribed of going to God, and divers practices of the spiritual life, I thought that this would serve rather to puzzle me than to facilitate what I sought after, which was nothing else but how to become wholly God's.' For him, the ' most excellent method . . . of going to God was that of doing our common business . . . purely for the love of God '; ' we ought to act with God in the greatest simplicity, speaking to him frankly and plainly, and imploring his assistance in our affairs, just as they happen.' He describes how, having ' spent the hours appointed for private prayer in thinking of God ' he then ' went to his work appointed in the kitchen . . . ; there, having first considered severally the things his office required, and when and how each thing was to be done, he spent all the intervals of his time, as well before as after his work, in prayer'; and ' when sometimes he had not thought of God for a good while, he did not disquiet himself for it; but after having acknowledged his wretchedness to God, he returned to him with so much the greater trust in him, by how much he found himself more wretched to have forgotten him.' And ' when we are faithful to keep ourselves in his holy presence . . . this not only hinders our offending him . . . but it also begets in us a holy freedom and, if I may so speak, a familiarity with God, wherewith we ask, and that successfully, the graces we stand in need of. In fine, by often repeating these acts, they become habitual and the presence of God is rendered as it were natural to us.'[1]

Here, indeed, there is no high drama, no epic grandeur: this is the way of God's little ones, the common way open to all; but the end is glory.

' At the end we shall be judged on love ': the human love we have been given to guard and cherish, the divine love which is enjoined upon us all. It is above all by loving God and man that we are called to imitate the creative Word: and if we do that, in however simple and lowly a fashion, we shall be creative of more than our own lives: we shall join with the Word in leading and welcoming humanity into the glow of that eternal hearth and home which is the heart of God.

[1] Bro Lawrence: *The Practice of the Presence of God.*

VIII

The Role of Woman

O F ALL the trends we have been considering as characteristic
of the world today—the increasing loss of wisdom and vision,
of stillness, of Nature, of the stability of home and family life, of
symbol—it seems true to say that they represent something particularly alien to the nature of woman.

Alien, indeed, to the feminine nature in all of us, men and women
alike: the argument has been precisely that our troubles spring
from the over-emphasis on the masculine in our world, the neglect
of the feminine. Why then, it might be asked, single out woman
in particular? Is she regarded as being particularly to blame? The
answer to this latter question is of course an emphatic no: nothing
could be more foolish, in any case, than to try to decide which of
the two sexes is the more to blame. . . . It is not a question here of
blame at all; but of opportunity. Precisely because the nature of
the psychological crisis through which we are passing is what it
is, woman has an unique opportunity to redeem the situation: she
can, if she is true to her deepest nature, come forward with immense
power to heal humanity, and in so doing achieve for herself an
immense glory. That is the burden of the present chapter.

It is the feminine *Philosophia* who leads Boethius to the feminine
Sophia, Sapientia, Wisdom; it is Beatrice who leads Dante to
vision; the most obvious characteristics of Mary the Mother of
God are her stillness and silence and her deep wisdom. By nature
woman is not activist but contemplative: in primitive society it is
the man who goes out to hunt, to adventure, to make war; it is

the woman, the conserver, who stays to guard the home. She is closer to Nature than is man: she learns through her body, and especially through motherhood, in a way he never can. He, with his cartesian desire for the clear and distinct idea, may be irritated, at the conscious level, by the ' untidiness ' of the language of symbol: she is more likely to find it her own language. You would suppose then that in an age like our own, when woman is playing a far more active part in the life of society than ever before, such trends would be checked rather than intensified: what is the explanation ?

The answer has already been suggested. Just at the very moment in history when the ' feminine ' was more urgently needed than ever before to right the balance of a hypertrophy of the masculine in humanity, woman has herself tended to become—partly through force of circumstances (the demands of war-time society), partly, it was suggested, through a misunderstanding of the idea of equality —more and more masculine. The wars forced on women the work, and to that extent the modes of thought, of men; the struggle for equality of rights turned to some extent into a struggle for equality, for an equality which would destroy the differences between the sexes, and to that extent damage humanity.

' When we observe,' writes Dr Jung, ' the way in which women since the second half of the nineteenth century, have begun to learn masculine callings, to become active in politics, to found and lead societies, etc., we can see that woman is in the process of breaking with the purely feminine sexual schema in which apparent unconsciousness and passivity play a leading role. She begins to concede something to masculine psychology by establishing herself as a visible member of society. . . . This step towards social independence is a symptom, even though it be only a response to compelling economic facts, and due to causes, other than the actual need itself. The courage and capacity for self-sacrifice of such women is certainly to be marvelled at, and only the blind could fail to see the good that has come out of these efforts. But no one can evade the fact that in taking up a masculine calling, studying, and working in a man's way, woman is doing something not wholly in agreement with, if not directly injurious to, her feminine nature. She is doing what would be scarcely possible for a man to do, even were he a Chinaman. Could he, for example, take a place as a governess, or be in charge of a kindergarten? When I speak of injury, I do not mean physiological merely, but above all psychic injury. It is a woman's outstanding characteristic that she can do everything for the love of a man. But those women who can achieve something important for the love of a thing are most exceptional, because this does not really agree with their nature. The love of a thing is man's prerogative.'[1]

Let us be quite clear: we are here in a sense dealing with abstractions. Nobody, of either sex, is one hundred per cent male or female: we are all psychologically bisexual, and the two elements co-exist in every personality in an infinite variety of proportions. And vocation is an individual affair. Thus there are many women who, psychologically speaking, are predominantly masculine, and who will find their vocation and their happiness in a 'masculine' career, just as there are many men who are predominantly feminine from the psychological point of view, and who will tend to find their vocation less in rational than in intuitive pursuits. But when all that is said, it remains true that on the whole man tends to be predominantly of one psychological type, and woman of another. The primitive difference between the man who is the active hunter, adventurer, bread-winner, warrior, on the one hand, and the woman who is the mother and conserver of the home and the family, on the other, continues psychologically into civilized society. The man adventures in ideas, in scientific discovery and invention: he is the builder, the legislator, concerned with the immediate needs of life, with the rational ordering of life, with the building up of what is new. The woman remains the conserver: keeping and 'pondering in her heart' the words, the experiences, which life brings, looking beyond the immediate to the ultimate, and

---

[1] C. G. Jung: *Contributions to Analytical Psychology*, p. 169.
Cp M. Thibon: 'Women think of the object of their love in the second person, they must always call him " you " . . . Only men can dedicate themselves to something that is never addressed but always referred to as " it." Women feel the need to speak *to* someone, men to speak *of* something.' (*What God has Joined Together*, p. 154.) And Jung: 'Woman is far more " psychological " than man. For the most part he contents himself with " logic " simply. Everything " psychical," " unconscious," etc., is antipathetic to him. It seems to him misty, vague, and pathological. He wants the actual thing, the fact, not the feelings or phantasies that hover around it. To the woman it is often more important to know how a man feels about a thing than to understand the thing itself.' (*Contributions to Analytical Psychology*, p. 178.)

thus gradually acquiring her rich store of intuitive wisdom.[1] 'Her psychology is founded on the principle of eros, the great binder and deliverer; while age-old wisdom has ascribed logos to man as his ruling principle.'[2] It is this that can render so arduous that search for mutual understanding which we were considering before: 'For the man, eros belongs to a shadowland; it entangles him in his feminine unconscious—the 'psychical'; while to the woman logos is a deadly, boring kind of sophistry, if she is not simply afraid of, and repelled by it.'[3] But it is precisely this difference too which, given that mutual understanding and sympathy, can make the union of the two psyches so immensely rich and fruitful.

'It may be said of woman,' writes Prof. Guitton, 'that her " hour is not yet come " in the history of the world, although many signs suggest the belief that that hour is not far distant. That is not to say that woman has not played a primordial role in the human past, a role all the more essential for its secrecy. Man rules on the surface of things. He is at home in tempests and at the crest of the waves. Woman, on the contrary, dwells in the depths.' And he goes on to argue that, for that very reason, 'the soul of woman is not concerned with history,' i.e. with events on the surface. But here his language would seem to be, to say the least, misleading. Even when we have emphasized once again that all this refers to the essential vocation of Woman-as-Type and not to this or that individual woman, it still seems untrue to say without qualification that because her vocation is to 'inspire and sympathize' (as indeed

[1] She must of course, as the psychologists put it, 'come to terms with her animus,' as must the man with his anima, if she is really to be wise. If the animus on the contrary takes possession of her she can be capable of being extremely foolish—and extremely tiresome—in the name of reason. Dr Jung remarks that ' the astonishing assumptions and phantasies that women have about men come from the activity of the animus, which is inexhaustible in the production of illogical judgements and false explanations of causes' (*Contributions*, p. 200); and Dr Eleanor Bertine, giving a vivid description of a man-woman wrangle in terms of anima and animus conflict, and noting that ' the animus may likewise precipitate the conflict,' points out how ' it may cause the woman to tell the man what he ought to do, or to make some generalized assumption, whose lack of validity is perfectly obvious to the man, yet upon which she pontificates with the most maddening assurance. This unrelated pseudo-thinking chills the atmosphere, producing an alienation of feeling which is greatly worsened by the dictatorial manner in which the pronouncements are made. Thus the two human beings do not really touch each other at all, but are separated by a thick barrier of blindly autonomous thoughts and feelings, arising from the unconscious ' (*Men and Women*, Guild of Pastoral Psychology, Lecture No. 60, p. 16).

[2] Jung: *op. cit.* pp. 175-6.

[3] Jung, *op. cit.* p. 177.

it is), her function therefore is not ' to appear in public,' and that
' she reigns in private.' The essential qualification must be added:
her function is not to appear in public, not to reign, in a *masculine*
mode or capacity. The woman who becomes the hard-faced and
hard-voiced boss, the virago-matriarch, will not save us; on the
other hand what we desperately need to-day is that Woman should
appear in public, should reign, *as such*: as Mary appeared in public
at the foot of the Cross, and reigns now as Queen of heaven. (It
is indeed precisely a happy augury for the future that at this present
time the British throne which, as a result of the constitutional
changes through the centuries, has ceased to exercise a ' masculine '
role, as it did for instance in the days of the Tudors, but has instead
assumed a ' feminine ' role which can have profound significance
and importance, should be occupied by a Queen Regnant.) When
all this has been said, however, it remains true that, as Prof. Guitton
concludes, ' Woman's being is more near to the nature of things.
Her role, when offered suffering, silence or glory, is to murmur:
" Let it be so." Her vocation is to wait, to suggest and respond,
to be far more than *to do*.'[1]

So to Mary in her stillness comes the announcement which is
the summons to both suffering and glory, and her reply is ' So be
it '; and her vocation henceforth is to live and work and suffer for
the fulfilment of *his* vocation; and she does not command or urge,
she suggests: ' they have no wine '; when the time comes for
him to ' go out into the world ' she retires into the background,
she waits; and when at the end he needs her comfort and her
strength she gives it, not by saying anything or doing anything,
but by standing silent at the foot of the cross, by *being* with him.

The role of woman is to suggest and inspire: not to act but to
inspire man to act; not to command and take the initiative, but
to empower him to command and take the initiative; not to save
him, but to give him the courage and strength and wisdom to save
himself. ' An important section of the " mythology of woman," '
writes Prof. Eliade, ' will prove that it is always a feminine being
who aids the hero to conquer immortality or to emerge victorious
from his initiation-testings.'[2]

[1] *Essay on Human Love*, pp. 221-4.   [2] *Mystique et Continence*, p. 44.

The trend today, in the role and status of woman, seems to be wholly away from all this; and what then are we to think of the future? 'It is not thus,' writes Prof. Guitton, 'that we picture the march of human development.' And he goes on to quote an interesting passage from Rilke, 'whose genius was so prophetic': 'The young girl and the woman will only for a time imitate masculine manners and modes in their own development, only for a time practise masculine professions. Once these fluctuating times of transition are at an end, it will be seen that women, in these often ridiculous masquerades, have only sought to purify their nature from the distorting influences of the other sex. Woman, who lives a more spontaneous, fertile, confident life, is certainly more mature, more near to the human than man, the pretentious and impatient male, blind to the worth of that which he thinks he loves, because he does not plumb the depths as woman does by reason of the burdensome fruit of life. . . . One day (to which certain signs in the Nordic countries already point) the maiden, the woman will come to her own . . . Such an advance will transform the experience of love, today so full of faults, and that in spite of man who will first be outstripped. Love will no longer be the intercourse of man with woman, but that of one humanity with another. (*Von Mensch zu Mensch, nicht mehr von Mann zu Weib.*) And this more human love (this love full of respect and silence, sound and sure in all that it binds and looses) is indeed that for which, in strife and pain, we make ready.'[1]

If woman, then, is to be true to her role today, it must be, not of course through abdicating her hard-won freedom, still less through rejecting her essential femininity, but by integrating the two together. And this process will once again involve the dark journey, a new birth. 'As a consequence of the development on the individual side of her nature,' writes Dr Eleanor Bertine, 'modern woman has partially lost contact with the archetypal Woman in herself. This should be her conscious principle, as her grandmother knew instinctively, and it seems ironic that she should have to learn the fact at all. Yet it is a common experience that those things which have been lived unconsciously since the beginning of time,

---

[1] *Essay on Human Love*, pp. 225-8.

may have to die, as automatic or natural responses, in order to be reborn as conscious, voluntary actions. This is probably even more true for women than for men, for the feminine psyche seems to be less centred in the head than the masculine, and so a rational understanding of the truths of its nature comes with more difficulty.'[1]

Such a development, however, according to Dr Bertine, is already coming to pass. ' Women have learned the value of freedom, not only for selfhood, but for the fullest expression of love . . . While men struggle with their own special problems in world politics, watched and often abetted by women, the latter are beginning to discover that something can be done, in their own realm of eros, to reintegrate the ways of nature and effect the archetypal union of Yang and Yin [i.e. of logos and eros] in human experience —but this time, on a more conscious level.'[2]

If this is true, it shows us among other things the immense importance today of a wise philosophy of education for girls and women. The evils which at present loom so large in the education of the male are doubly evil when they are found in the education of the female. The primary purpose here must surely be to educe and deepen the intuitive life of woman, her womanly wisdom. The time spent (or wasted) in school on chemistry or trigonometry would be better employed in opening to the girl, in a feminine way, the world of poetry, of the fine (and domestic) arts; in religious instruction, similarly the emphasis should be put on the world of religious symbols, on the wisdom of the saints and mystics, on the art of prayer. Rational training of course there must be, in religion and in secular culture alike; but always translated as far as possible into terms of the concrete, the personal, the particular. Thus, dogma must be transposed into a direct awareness of the reality behind the dogma, into an intuitive grasp of the corresponding symbols, and into an awareness of the correspondence between the supernatural reality and natural values. The mystery of the Incarnation, for instance, can be linked up with the human feminine mystery of child-birth, with the rebirth of humanity, with all the content of the mother-symbol; for woman is herself the symbol of rebirth and renewal, and she will understand the divine renewal of humanity

[1] Eleanor Bertine, *op. cit.*   [2] *ibid.*

if it is conveyed to her in terms which chime with the facts of her own destiny, of her own body and soul, with the way in which, through her body, the Word is (analogously) to be made flesh in her own children who, it will be her business to make sure, are ' to be called the children of God.'

For today, as yesterday, as always, the ideal Woman is the Mother of God; and today as always the vocation of every woman is in one way or another to imitate her, to share in her vocation as the mother of men. But to do that she will need also to share in the doubly rich personality of Mary who is both virgin and mother: she will need the wisdom that comes of experience, the wisdom a woman learns through her body, and in particular through her motherhood; but at the same time she will need the other wisdom, the virginal wisdom of the girl, the feminine counterpart to the ' grace and truth ' of the *Puer aeternus*.[1]

Put into ethical terms, this latter wisdom means the insight, the sense of the true and the good, the faculty of intuitive judgment, which come not from experience of evil but precisely from inexperience of evil: from remaining unspoilt. So innocence will sense the approach of evil not because it has known it before but precisely because it is unfamiliar and alien. So it will point it out, and shun it, because it will be conscious of its discordance; just as it will at once recognize goodness because of its own connaturality with goodness.

But if the innocence is lost? It can be recovered. St Peter was made familiar with evil when he denied his Master; but through his sorrow for the evil he learned anew the mercy of God, and through that new knowledge he learned as never before to love God: and in that love it was God who became familiar to him, and evil that receded from him and became alien to him.

This is again a dark journey; but it is one which must indeed be creative for a woman who is to become, with Mary, a mother of men. One of the greatest glories of Mary is her making known to us, in her own personality, of the motherhood of God. We are taught by our Lord to think of God, and to address God, as our Father: it is no doubt because we need the sense of awe, which the

---

[1] I have treated this idea more fully in *The Seven Swords*, ch. I.

concept of motherhood does not elicit in the same way; moreover, were we to think of God in terms of motherhood alone we might more easily form a radically erroneous idea of what that motherhood should mean for us, and might fall into the pseudo-religion of escape, of protection from life, of petting and rest. But it remains true that the concept of fatherhood is not intended to exclude the qualities we associate more especially with mother-love: the gentleness, sympathy, understanding, tenderness—is it not indeed precisely such qualities as these which are implicit in our Lord's likening of himself to the hen gathering her chickens under her wing?

A mother understands her children in a way that nobody else can: she understands them through her body, they are part of her, and so she has literally a sympathy, a co-suffering, with them, not only in their trials and sorrows but in their sins and follies as well. She cannot be shocked, because she is never surprised or uncomprehending: she knows. And this quality in God's love and mercy is something which we need to understand today especially, when there is so much evil and folly, so much hatred and cruelty and squalor, in the world. Men who will not look for God in his heaven may yet find him in their own private hell, in the agony of their hearts, in the agony of their world. We need to know redemption in its living reality: the reality of God's descent into our squalors and miseries so as to search for us and find us and save us there. It is this that Mary, the Refuge of Sinners, shows us.

Thus the idea of these present times as initiating an 'age of Mary,' in which her personality, her influence, and the influence of all that she symbolizes for humanity, will loom larger than ever before, is seen to coincide with that view of history which regards our own age as a period in which ultimate Reality is rediscovered, not (as in earlier times) as a purely transcendent deity, nor as purely immanent, humanity itself the measure of all things, but as both immanent and transcendent: transcendent because indeed the *Mysterium Tremendum*, but immanent because made flesh, and made flesh in order to share the sorrows and squalors of flesh.

'The eyes of the saint,' writes Fr Thomas Merton, 'make all beauty holy, and the hands of the saint consecrate everything they touch to the glory of God, and the saint is never offended by any-thing and is scandalized by no man's sin because he does not know sin.' The first part of the sentence was quoted earlier; but in fact the two parts hang together: the saint consecrates and sanctifies *because* he is never offended or scandalized (i.e. led into sin himself): and he is never offended or scandalized because he does not know sin, i.e. he has the motherly qualities of Mary because he has—or, having lost, has recovered—the virginal qualities of Mary, her strangeness to sin. If woman, then, is to share in the motherhood of Mary she must share in these qualities. She must have the unspoilt freshness of heart, the untarnished vision, of Mary the Girl: she must also have the deep, compassionate wisdom and gentleness of Mary the Mother. She will need to be brave enough and strong enough to go down into humanity's squalors, and travail there for humanity's rebirth.

And in so doing she will not only be helping man to find his own destiny; she will be fulfilling her own. For without this, what might she become? She might, at the other extreme, become one of those women 'who despise their irrationality and are ashamed of being riddles to man' and so 'become unapproachable virgins or blue-stockings, career-women or viragos.' She might become one of the *femmes fatales* who are 'merely proud of their enigmatic ways and moods and revel in these anima-tricks' and do not 'acknowledge their deeper *need* of men,' and so become 'something like fairies or will-o'-the-wisps or Helenas in whose life innumerable sex experiences may take place or none at all without this making much difference to them, because in the depth of their being these women are never really committed.'[1] She might become a mother indeed, but the enveloping, possessive, destructive mother like the Borgia princess in the story recounted by Dr Bertine, who, 'night after night put a drop of poison into her lover's soup, and, day by day, won the wonder and admiration of the court by wearing herself to skin and bone in her indefatigable ministering to him: . . . she had to reduce him to being all hers, like a helpless child, before she could pour out her tenderness upon him.'[2]

[1] Eva Metman: *Woman and the Anima* (Guild of Pastoral Psychology, Lecture No. 71).
[2] Eleanor Bertine, *op. cit.*

If she is to be true both to her age-long destiny and to her new-found freedom, it must be by accepting consciously and deliberately her redemptive role and preparing herself consciously and deliberately for it by imitating the Mother of men. In all ages women have been driven by the blind, instinctive urge of love to share the hell of the men they love: perhaps woman's new consciousness will now give that sharing a new purposiveness and a new efficacy.

'Our abstract and violent culture,' writes Prof. Guitton, 'oscillating ceaselessly between the most subtle speculation and the most cruel of conflicts (when it does not combine them), is confronted with this dilemma: either to destroy itself or to return to its sources. This return to simplicity, to nature, to humanity, to being, to a truth commensurate with the heart, to the union of the mystical, the reasonable and the practicable, will undoubtedly come to pass under the pressure of diverse influences: and among them that of woman might well be preponderant. Goethe thought that the masculine monad was often more rich and productive than the contrary; but, he said, since it desires to realize its content while carrying it to full consciousness and by a definite act of will, it is extremely subject to error and disturbance, while the feminine monad is spontaneously orientated towards equilibrium; still more, she draws man towards a celestial realm, she redeems him. . . . It may be that the new Adam, the man of the age to come, may, not after the flesh but after the spirit, come from the thought of woman who is alone capable of readaptation to nature and of re-establishing the equilibrium of a restless being fashioned for creation, criticism and revolt.'[1]

Charles Williams, in his *Religion and Love in Dante*, underlines the significance of the moment in the *Paradiso* when 'for the first time in the whole history' Dante forgets Beatrice altogether. She has cried out to him: *Ringrazia, ringrazia* . . . 'give thanks, give thanks to the Sun of the Angels'; and Dante is 'so moved by devotion at these words, and by desire for God' that he forgets her; but she, 'she is so delighted at this that she laughs at the heavenly infidelity, and " the splendour of her laughing eyes "

[1] *op. cit.* pp. 229-230.

catches his mind back from the vision (for which he is not yet ready) —to her? no, but to the glowing lights about him which are the great doctors of the Church.' Later on, ' there follows the profound and mystical final substitution. The eyes of Beatrice have been the sign and means of ascent in experience; they have shown themselves to Dante and in a sense known heaven for Dante. But at the moment when " Beatrice and all the blessed " implore the Divine Mother for him, it is not her eyes that the poem names, though it may be her eyes also that the poem means. It is Mary's— " those eyes, loved and venerated by God." It is the mortal maternity of Godhead that is here expressed. But this also is not alien from the Way: what else had Beatrice seemed when she came after Joan in the mortal city? '[1]

In the Litany of Loretto we salute Mary as Seat of Wisdom, Tower of Ivory, Consoler of the Distressed, Refuge of Sinners: as wise and strong, as tender and compassionate. She gives her strength and her joy to Jesus the Baby; she gives her strength and her compassion to the Humiliated Christ. The harassed, restless, neurotic masculine world of today needs the divine motherhood as never before; and needs the human mystery of woman's motherhood as never before. And it needs the second to lead it back to the first.

'Who is this,' we read in the *Song of Songs*, ' whose coming shows as the dawn of day? No moon so fair, no sun so majestic, no embattled array so awes men's hearts.' And the Church applies the words to Mary, the Queen of heaven and of earth. But it is that beauty, that majesty, which goes down into the dust with the Sun of Angels in his agony. If woman is faithful to her nature, to her own feminine beauty and wisdom and majesty, she will continue to inspire man to great deeds. But if she is tender as well as beautiful, humble as well as strong, compassionate as well as wise, and if in the strength of her humility and compassion she is not afraid to imitate God and search for man in his squalors, then she will fulfil her own vocation in all its glory, and she will do much more for man than inspire him with dreams of greatness: she will redeem him.

[1] *op. cit.* pp. 36, 39.

IX

The Recovery of Nature

'CAIN, who killed his brother Abel, the herdsman,' wrote Dr
Coomaraswamy, ' and built himself a city, prefigures modern
civilization, one that has been described from within as " a murder-
ous machine, with no conscience and no ideals," " neither human
nor normal nor christian," and in fact " an anomaly, not to say a
monstrosity." It has been said: " The values of life are slowly
ebbing. There remains the show of civilization, without any of its
realities." Criticisms such as these could be cited without end.
Modern civilization, by its divorce from any principle, can be
likened to a headless corpse of which the last motions are convulsive
and insignificant.'[1]

It is a good thing for us to remind ourselves sometimes of how
we look to the rest of the world. Dr Coomaraswamy quotes a
pronouncement by Sir George Watt in 1912 that ' however much
Indian art may be injured, or individuals suffer, progression in line
with the manufacturing enterprise of civilization must be allowed
free course.' ' In the same year,' he continues, ' Gandhi said that
" India is being ground down, not under the English heel, but under
that of modern civilization." In an open letter to Gilbert Murray,
the late Rabindranath Tagore said, " There is no people in the
whole of Asia which does not look upon Europe with fear and
suspicion." . . . A speaker at Boston College lately described modern
western civilization as a " curse to humanity." '[2] But the idea of

[1] Ananda K. Coomaraswamy: *Am I My Brother's Keeper?* p. 1. The authors quoted
are: G. La Piana, in *Harvard Divinity School Bulletin*, xxvii; Eric Gill, *Autobiography*; René
Guénon, *East and West*; A. N. Whitehead, *Adventures of Ideas*.

[2] *op. cit.* pp. 2-3.

the ' white man's burden ' dies hard: surely, with all our faults we do bring ' progress ' to other races: we do alleviate their poverty by industrialization and their ignorance by teaching them to read and write? Yes, but at what cost? ' An incessant " progress," never ending in contentment, means the condemnation of all men to a state of irremediable poverty. In the words of St Gregory Nazazien,

> ' *Could you from all the world all wealth procure,*
> *More would remain, whose lack would leave you poor!* '

As for reading and writing, if they are ' to enable the Indian and Chinese masses to read what the western proletariat reads, they will remain better off, from any cultural point of view, with their own more classical literature of which they all have oral knowledge . . . It is still true that, as Sir George Birdwood wrote in 1880, " Our education has destroyed their love of their own literature . . . It has disgusted them with their own homes—their parents, their sisters, their very wives. It has brought discontent into every family so far as its baneful influences have reached." ' [1]

We may remind ourselves, moreover, as Dr Coomaraswamy's deadly indictment goes on, that he knew our civilization from within as well as from without, and was very far from having any hatred of it in his heart; on the contrary. But he puts our own problem for us succinctly. How can ' this extraverted mentality be awakened, reminded of itself, and converted from its senti-mentality and its sole reliance on estimative knowledge to the life of the intellect? How can this world be given back its meaning? Not, of course, by a return to the outward forms of the Middle Ages nor, on the other hand, by assimilation to any surviving, Oriental or other, pattern of life. But why not by a recognition of the principles on which the patterns were based? These principles, on which the " unspoiled " life of the east is still supported, must at least be grasped, respected, and understood if ever the western provincial is to become a citizen of the world.' [1]

This book has been concerned, so far, with suggestions as to ways in which we might ' recover our roots ' and so return to

[1] *ibid.*   [2] *op. cit. p. 10.*

health and sanity. But it would seem likely that any such recovery, apart from isolated individual efforts, must remain impracticable so long as the general structure of life as it is lived in the great cities, in our industrialized, technological society, remains as it is: remote from Nature, remote from the earth, wrapped up in cellophane . . .

There can be no question of abolishing industrialism : the problem is to discover how industrialism can be changed, can be ' humanized,' in such a way that it will be possible once again for man to claim his fundamental natural right to be creative in his work and independent and secure in his home. There are certain ways and means which would help to this end: in economics, for instance, the principle of devolution in industry; in politics, the principle of the distribution of property instead of the State-concentration of property; but such means will never be adequately worked out, still less applied, until there is a sufficiently vehement demand for them: and how is that demand to be created? The cellophane age creates cellophane personalities; the cellophane personalities in their turn acquiesce in the cellophane age: how is the vicious circle to be broken into?

The one hope lies in the fact that human nature dies hard. The acquiescence may be apparently complete but it remains relatively superficial: deep down underneath the surface the essential needs and demands of human nature live on, and find, no doubt, plenty of queer and baneful outlets by way of substitute for their proper fulfilment. But if the nature of that proper fulfilment were consciously recognized, would anything stop the achievement of it?

Man is an animal: his roots are in Nature, in the earth. That is not to say that he needs, for his own personal fulfilment, to be a farmer or a gardener or to live in the country; but it does mean that if he lives in a city it must be a ' natural ' city, where he is in contact with Nature none the less, with green and growing things, with the rhythm of the cosmos. For to be on the contrary ' cut off ' from the cosmos is a thing far more likely to happen to man than to woman, who is biologically so much nearer to mother-earth.

' Because of her body woman is subject to the drama of existence. When she is not bearing children her organs have their periods

related to the rhythm of the cosmos which bring the cadence of
the stars and the phases of the moon into her life. Just as the blossoming of spring reminds the inhabitants of the earth that their planet
revolves round the sun, so the menstrual periods link woman to
the universe. She is thus subject to the respiration of nature and
the chain of causality. It is in her womb that the race rises again
at each birth and it is often in her arms that it dies. Though she is
detached from history, she is attached to life, which is more leisurely
and more profound than history.'[1]

Man for his part, then, stands in special need of awareness of
and communion with the ' blossoming of spring,' the autumn fall,
the winter death. It is good and important for him to grow things
with his own hands, just as it is good and important for him to
make things with his own hands. We can be profoundly grateful
for the continuing vigour of the instinct which urges men to have
and keep their own garden and, if they cannot have a garden, at
least to have an ' allotment.'

But supposing that he is debarred by force of circumstances
even from that? There are still the occasional contacts, the ' days
in the country,' in which relationship may be established; there
are all the ways also of learning indirectly, from the poets and
painters, from films and from books: ways not of learning about
Nature but of learning Nature.

But how convince a man that he *needs* this sort of contact, this
awareness and communion? If he is not to be convinced by dis-
cussion he may yet be convinced by example: his neighbour's
obvious joy and fulfilment in his plot of land may induce him to
try conclusions with his own. The question, Why are you so
happy?—if it is real happiness and not the boisterous and hollow
bonhomie of retarded development—is always interesting to the
frustrated man. But if all this fails there may still be hope; for the
connexion between the natural and the creative is very close; and
if a man can be brought to see that the only sane and healthy life
is the creative life—and to contrast such a life with the uncreative-
ness of the cellophane existence—he may then be brought to see
also that it is uncreative *because* it is unnatural, and that if he is to

[1] J. Guitton: *op. cit.* p. 222.

reclaim his birthright in the one case he must first of all reclaim it in the other.

Omnia per ipsum facta sunt: the instinct to imitate the creative Word, to be a maker, goes very deep. When all else fails, you find it expressed in pathetic, etiolated form, in the man who likes to 'tinker' in his spare time, having no other form of making at his disposal. If a man is to be fulfilled he must be a maker of one sort or another in his work; to be perfectly fulfilled he must also be able to be a maker of one sort or another in his play. But this already implies a certain naturalness, because a certain natural contemplation. Just as the modern poet may write of jet-planes and sky-scrapers and the hum of mighty machinery, but beneath there is the consciousness of the earth, of the steady rhythm of life, of the stillness beneath the noise; so too with the humbler forms of making. The man who loves making things out of wood (whether the making be his vocation or his avocation) will be, at least as far as wood is concerned, a contemplative: the feel of wood will be in his fingers, and he will treat his materials with reverence: and here at least, in consequence, he will be able to see that the good is the natural: he will be able to see that art which is not rooted in Nature becomes either degraded, like the demented horrors of 'fret-work,' or a complete travesty, like those garden benches in which iron was tortured to look like rustic wood. And if he can see that art without Nature is a travesty, he may then go on to see that life without Nature is a travesty.

For indeed it is not in his work only that man is meant to be creative; it is in his life as a whole.

Morality, for instance, in the christian view is doubly creative: in itself as the 'integration of the personality,' and as being a function of religion and therefore a creative act of love of God. It is easy enough to show that evil disintegrates the personality (as in *Dorian Gray*); what we have to do is to go on to show that goodness integrates the personality. The 'Do not' is there only for the sake of the 'Do': and that in its turn only for the sake of the 'Be.' To forbid disintegration is to command its opposite. To paint the christian life merely in terms of the avoidance of evil, the eradiction of sinful impulses, is to miss its whole meaning. The

saint is flame, not snow. No man can live in a vacuum. When
the house was swept and garnished the devil returned, bringing
with him seven other devils. . . . The conquering of sin is either the
negative aspect of the discovery of love or there is nothing specifically
christian, or indeed religious, about it at all. The commandments
of the Old Law express the negative minimum: the christian law
of love expresses the positive ideal. Not only shall you not kill or
steal or commit adultery, but, if you would live the christian life
in its fullness, you must go beyond the mere respecting of the lives
and properties and homes of others: you must be ready if need be
to lay down your life for others, to give up your own property
when others are in need, perhaps to sacrifice a family life of your
own for a yet greater good. The end in view, the complete integration, is, as we have seen, not virtue merely but holiness, not prose
merely but poetry: not conformity to a pattern merely but the
creation of a pattern, a creation in which man is directed by the
Spirit that ' bloweth where it listeth ' and that gives to the christian
life in its fullness that unexpectedness and spontaneity, that lyrical
quality and sense of effortless power, which are to be found so
markedly and sometimes so dramatically in the lives of the saints.

To be holy is to be in the deepest sense natural, because holiness
includes the fulfilment of human nature. Evil on the other hand is
unnatural, because it is disruptive of nature: of human nature in
the first place, but also, in the long run, of the *ordo universi*, the
whole scheme of things. We live in a twisted world. It is sympto-
matic of the pass to which we have come that the abuse of Nature,
the creation of ugliness, is no longer regarded as a sin at all. Quite
apart from its direct sins against human beings, industrialism is
steeped in sin because of the way it destroys the earth. It is a terrible
sin to build a slum, to befoul the rivers, to strip the forests, to kill
beauty everywhere and to erect everywhere monuments of ugliness,
monuments to the greed and blindness and vulgarity of man. It is
a crime against Nature, a crime against humanity: it is also a
crime against the relationship between the two; for man should
be helped to vision and to holiness by his environment, but the
more unnatural you make that environment and the more you
fill it with ugliness and noise and squalor, the more impossible you

make the kind of atmosphere in which holiness is encouraged to be created and to flourish.

If work is meant to be creative, and morality is meant to be creative, still more obviously love must be creative, and still more obviously to drag it away from its natural roots is to destroy it. The cellophane age makes love a predominantly cerebral thing: it inculcates the cult of glamour, of sex-appeal, and so it degrades physical beauty just as surely as it ignores any other sort of beauty —for physical beauty cannot receive the honour which is its due if it is isolated (either in the beholder or in the possessor) from the human personality as a whole. The cellophane age encourages girls to think of themselves as budding Liliths, and young men to groom themselves to play Casanova; for the more unnatural the setting, the more unnatural the attitude to love will be. 'In the realm of love, the words of Walt Whitman are particularly appropriate, "Only the kernel nourishes." Only those human beings who bring their deepest, inmost reality to love can have any experience of its true joy and fulfilment. This is often forgotten by those modern young people who think that they know all about love because they have had a fine salad of erotic experience. Actually, what they cynically call their realism is only a cloak for a complete ignorance of everything below the surface. They have been too greedy for pleasure, too unwilling to face pain, or just too unawakened to stand up against the drift in their social set, ever to be able to deserve anything but the anger of the god of love. As Kahlil Gibran says in *The Prophet*:

" *For even as love crowns you, so shall he crucify you.*

. . . .

He threshes you to make you naked.
He sifts you to free you from husks.
He grinds you to whiteness.
He kneads you till you are pliant.

. . . .

But if, in your fear, you would seek only love's peace and love's
 pleasure,

*Then it is better for you that you cover your nakedness and pass out
of love's threshing-floor,
Into the seasonless world where you shall laugh, but not all of your
laughter, and weep, but not all of your tears." '[1]*

Human society again is meant to be a creative thing: the
common creation of a common life; but, as we have seen already,
community dies when organization replaces organism; and
organism is dependent on a sense of a common earth, a common
patria, as the basis of a blood-tie which lives and is operative underneath all the differentiations of caste or class or function. But
where there is no such community the way is open to all sorts of
destructive surrogates: to mass hysteria and demagogy, to movements of the Hitler Youth type on the one hand or the relentless
hilarity of the organized 'holiday camp' on the other. It is not
in these and kindred ways that the lost sense of community will be
recovered[2]; but again if the loss itself is recognized as such it may
lead to an investigation of the causes of the loss, and to an appreciation of the fact that, once again, an unnatural society is in the end
a regimented collectivity in which creativeness cannot flourish.

It is one thing to criticize the world of industrialism from without; it is quite another to see its horror and yet to enter it and
attempt to redeem it from within. The modern apostolate of the
'priest-worker,' who does just this, must command our profound
admiration and respect. Here are men who devote themselves,
sacrifice themselves, to the task of re-humanizing an inhuman state
of affairs, of trying to teach men to be human so as to be able to
lead them on thence to the life which is divine—but to teach them,
not by preaching at them, but by living their lives and sharing
their poverties and their problems, their rootlessness and their
frustration.

What lies behind this new form of apostolate? ' At the base of
it all is the discovery of a world of men who no longer have any
spiritual link with the Church . . . the world which industrial
civilization has brought into bondage in every clime and in all
countries . . . Now this world is an atheistic world; not even a

---

[1] Eleanor Bertine, *op. cit.*
[2] Cf. *infra*, ch. X.

dechristianized world, for it has never been christian, but really and truly an atheistic world: the world of the factory essentially, but also the world of scientific research. Such a world was formed in the hey-day of liberalism, knowing nothing of any concern for religion. Moreover, such a world must not be confused with the world of communism, as one is sometimes too easily apt to confuse it. It was already atheistic before communism came into it and in some sort supplied it with a philosophy. Between such a world and that which the Church still reaches *there is no point of contact*.[1]

There is no point of contact: what then is to be done? how can any form of apostolate be initiated? The priest-workers as a whole are not concerned simply to ' go and preach in working-class districts just as others go and preach in bourgeois or rural districts ' —what good is preaching when there is no point of contact? Their concern is first ' to establish a contact and ensure a presence, that of Christ.' ' In such a milieu the presence of a priest is the sole means of re-establishing contact between the Church and the people, but it is obvious, too, that in such an atmosphere, at any rate at the beginning, the priest cannot express himself in sacramental acts for they would not be understood even in the smallest degree.' Once again, then, what is he to do? To establish his own contact, yes, but how is he to ' ensure the presence '? A passage from a novel on the subject by M. Gilbert Cesbron provides an answer by describing the sort of change which can take place.

' " The fresh confidence of men in each other, mutual help, reconciliations, the unity which up to now has been found only in the political struggle. . . . Almost every evening they drop in on one or the other, first of all talking about politics or the syndicates —old habits persist!—but when Pierre talks of other things, he's listened to in a different spirit. There's one new dweller at Sagnu —Christ. . . . What's wanted is to be with them, continually, in the work at its hardest and at closest quarters. . . ." As P. Pierre says to his archbishop in the dramatic conversation at the book's close, what the men see is the Gospel lived; " the neighbourhood begins to stir." '[1]

[1] Cf. *Priest-Workmen in France Today*, Blackfriars, Nov. 1952.
[2] Cf. Blackfriars, *loc. cit.*

Is it fanciful to suggest that the first fruit of the new ' contact,' the contact with a really *human* being, in this milieu is to produce (once the note of confidence is struck, and the relationship of unity, of mutual help, established) the first stirrings of a passionate interest precisely in the human,[1] and that this interest in the human provides just that ' point of contact' which had been lacking and without which any approach to religious concepts seems to be foredoomed to the failure of complete incomprehension?

Whatever the answer to that particular question may be, of one thing there can be no doubt. The old adage which bids us not to preach to the starving but to give them bread would mean in the present context that we are not to preach to the psychologically starving but are to give them the psychological bread of life: give them some hint as to how to become fully alive. If one is asked today, in the sort of milieu we are considering (and no doubt still more in the sort of ' bourgeois' milieu which is yet more sub-human because more mindless and less healthily animal) what one believes or believes in, it is surely useless to reply at once with a recital of the creeds or the catechism: they will mean nothing at all. The first thing is not to say, We believe in grace, redemption, the sacramental system, but to say in effect: We believe in living life fully and deeply; we believe in living creatively; we believe that only so long as we remain rooted in nature and in the rhythm of the universe, living always in touch with real things, natural things, the fundamental human realities of love, sex, hearth, soil, seasons, can we be really and creatively alive: creative in our work, in our life, in our homes, creative of a sane and wise and beautiful civilization. We believe that if we are imprisoned in an unnatural environment we must make a natural enclave for ourselves, in our own hearts, our own homes. We believe in seeing and treating human beings as real people, not as units or cogs in a machine, because we believe in the reality of the human family. We believe that one of our greatest treasures, which we must

[1] Of course the vast majority of men remain indestructibly human no matter what their circumstances (though the veritable army of trained thugs and torturers, at Belsen and elsewhere show us all too clearly how human beings can in fact be de-naturized, even *en masse*). But the word ' human ' used twice in the above sentence is used to mean ' living a human life in all its fullness and richness ' and ' that which makes a life fully and deeply human ' in a way which such a milieu makes difficult and perhaps impossible.

guard at all costs no matter what demands the superficial affairs of life thrust upon us, no matter how powerful our environment in seeking to rob us of it, is our faculty of wonder, our awareness of reality, our vision. . . .

If you said all this and it were untrue you would be quickly unmasked; but if you said it and it were true, a really and deeply, and above all a supernaturally, lived truth, its truth would be evident in your own personality—and would be of the kind that makes men free by inspiring them to liberate themselves. And then, but only then, you could begin to go further. You could begin to show how the human things point beyond themselves, how the window of life opens on to infinite horizons; at the same time you could begin to show how in the world of today there is only one great influence in the western world which is concerned to defend these human things and to teach men to treasure and defend them, and that that is christianity. In a world which grows more and more impersonal, where men are treated more and more ruthlessly as hands and cogs and regimented with less and less regard for their individual personalities, it is christianity which continues to assert that we must treat all men not merely as human beings even but as our brothers. In a world which is becoming more and more artificial and remote from natural things, it is christianity which constantly recalls us to those natural things, to our roots in the universe; it is christianity which uses and blesses the stone, the wood, the bread, the wine, the water, the oil, and in so doing teaches us incidentally to treasure and to understand the great basic human realities of love and sex, of home and hearth, of friendship and hospitality, of soil and seasons and sun and stars. It is christianity which keeps alive in us the faculty of wonder and tries to make us, even naturally speaking, contemplatives. It is christianity which teaches us to be still and look and listen to the ' essences of things '; which teaches men and women to have wonder for each other; which bids us join in the *Benedicite*, creation's song of praise. In a world which is like a ' headless corpse of which the last motions are convulsive and insignificant ' it is christianity which keeps us from becoming blind and desiccated materialists and utilitarians by reminding us all the time that we live in a sphere whose horizons are infinite and whose atmosphere is mystery.

Suppose the priest-worker for his part to have gathered about him in his slum-room a little group of christians, neophytes, others who would listen to him; suppose that he is about to celebrate Mass there, and wants first to talk to them: what would he say? Only the priest himself, of course, could answer that question; but it is perhaps permissible to speculate about what he *might* with advantage say, because one thing in the setting leaps to the eye: the fact that he and his hearers have immediately before them a contrast which is itself an eloquent lesson, and which is not offered, at least in the same degree, to the normal congregation in the normal church: the contrast between the ugly unreality of the world immediately outside the window, and the lovely reality of the things the priest is about to use and to do in an Act which is stripped of all but its barest essentials and carried out so near to the little group around him that they can really see and assimilate and understand.

What, then, he might say to them would perhaps be in substance, and differently expressed, something like this[1]:

'If you look out of the window there, you can see nothing but factory and tenement buildings; down there in the grey street there are children who have never heard the soft lapping of the sea or seen a meadow filled with buttercups or felt the clean wind sweeping across the hills; all around us there are men and women who have grown up like that and who have lost touch with reality because they are severed from their roots; almost you could say they have ceased to be part of the universe and when a man ceases to be that he ceases to be a human being in any full sense. Modern man has used his intellect to great effect within certain narrow limits; but he has lost the instinctive life, the intuitive life: he has no symbols. Once you lose the water and the wood, the wine, the oil; once you make love a question of sophisticated glamour and work a question of a dull uncreative routine; once, in other words, you forget your roots in human nature, in mother-earth, in the

---

[1] The 'discourse' which follows is adapted from an article, *The Bread of Life*, in The Life of the Spirit, Aug.-Sept. 1951.

cosmos, you doom yourself (or are doomed) to unreality. For the unnatural is the unreal. Even the christian who forgets the graciousness of nature forgets in the end the naturalness of grace, and finds himself in a sort of spiritual vacuum.

'Man is reason; but he is also instinct, intuition, emotion. Why go to Mass? people sometimes ask; and one answer which is very relevant today is that the Mass is, among other things, God's way of making us even naturally speaking sane and healthy.

'Look at this table on which the Mass will be offered: I helped to make it myself, on the farm where I was born, and you can feel the goodness of it, the grain is a joy to the eye; this bread, these hosts, were made by my sister from the corn that grows there, green and then gold and then white; and the wine too is from our own hillside and if I hold it up like this the great leonine sun gives it, even in our dun grey world, a new glory; and here is the cup we shall use, the great wide hospitable cup to show that man can try to be generous to copy the infinite generosity, the prodigality, of God.

'If you lived here in this slum, in these conditions, and knew no God, you know how lack-lustre, how hollow, how meaningless, your life could become. The Church teaches us to be human. Perhaps in one way we are lucky to meet together like this in this little room, away from all the pomp and beauty of the great churches, the great cathedrals, where things are done with such complicated ceremony and at such a distance from you that you may forget what exactly is being done.[1] The Church teaches us to be human: you need the soil, the trees, the water, you need the rhythm of

---

[1] Is it wrong to build magnificent churches in a world in which want and penury are still widespread? If we are tempted to answer quite bluntly, Yes, we should hesitate: shall we not be echoing the cry of indignation which comes down to us from the Gospel: This ointment might have been sold for three hundred pieces of silver, and alms might have been given to the poor? One of the things the modern world finds it hardest to understand —the world in which nothing is worth doing unless it is useful, and in which ' time is money '—is that man cannot live, and indeed in the last resort does not *want* to live, on bread alone.

The church is the house of God; and to embellish it is to honour God. The poor who love God will be anxious to do this, even at cost of great sacrifice to themselves. The nineteenth-century Russian Bishop Ignaty wrote: ' The people are pressed like ants in their poor huts, but they would build a high and beautiful temple of God. . . . they walk almost in rags, but they long to see the church shining with gold and silver.' And there is another aspect, suggested by another writer, Leskov: ' Do not prevent the living people of holy Russia from hoping and loving in a splendid church ' for while their own houses are, as

nature, you need real and deep contact with the real, fundamental things.

' In a healthy world men would not have to learn these things. But ours is a very unhealthy world; and we have to start again from the very beginning and be taught how to be human. *Quasi modo geniti*: like infants; and so it is only fitting that our Mother the Church should teach us. But this is a lesson that cannot be taught by appealing simply to the reason: it goes deeper than reason; and while the Church does indeed try to instruct our rational minds, it also has other and deeper lessons for us, it tries to form us as well as inform us, it tries to fit us back into the universe, to make us live the deep human and natural realities, and so come gradually to understand divine things not merely with our minds but with our whole personalities.

' Soon we shall kneel, join our hands in prayer, cross ourselves: these are all ways in which the Church teaches us to gather together the whole personality in strength and recollection, and enter the realm of eternal reality. We shall offer the bread and the wine to God, and with them we shall put our own lives and the lives of those we love and the needs of all the human family and all God's creation, that they may all be made holy; and then we shall listen as bread and wine are changed into God; and finally, at the table, we shall receive the God who thus takes possession of us.

' Why go to church? Because in the first place, quite apart from the immensities of grace and eternity, you will learn there how to receive reality, how to become real, how to live, for these are the living waters for lack of which the modern world is dying.

' The valley where this corn grew and was ground and made

Nadejda Gorodetzky puts it, ' but a night lodging of a pilgrim,' the church is ' the reflection of eternal life and bliss ' (Gorodetzky: *The Humiliated Christ in Modern Russian Thought*, p. 96).

But the church is built, not only to the glory of God, but also for the use and instruction of the faithful, to answer their needs; and today, when those needs are so basic and so critical, it may well be argued that the one over-riding aim in modern church-building must be to focus attention upon, and make possible the sight and assimilation of, the great realities of the Mass and the sacramental life—to reproduce, that is, so far as may be the immediacy and consequent sense of reality of the slum room of today's industrial city, the ' hiding-hole ' of the times of persecution in England, the catacombs of the early christians. The essential is that the Mass should not be a far-off spectacle but an *actio* (as the Canon of the Mass is called) in which all are near enough to share and which all, therefore, can absorb and assimilate.

into bread, where this wine was trodden in the press: how remote it seems from us here, and how unreal this world of ours seems by comparison. . . . There is no reason why life in the city should be cut off from these things, on the contrary; but in our case there is no question about it. And so we have to learn again, like little children; have to look and listen and feel, have to learn the blade of grass, the ear of corn, the stream, the sky, the stars; have to learn the great fundamental symbols, learn them consciously first of all, but in order that the lesson may sink deep and become part of us. We go to church to learn the Church's even natural wisdom, and to *become* that knowledge by living it, constantly, in the acts of worship.

' So in the Mass, the greatest of all symbols, we learn to live, we learn to be wise; and then we learn to understand, long for, receive not only the fullness of human life, but the life which is divine; and so we return to our roots not only in the universe but in God.

' Through the bread and wine we become rooted again in nature; through the bread and wine we begin to live a divine life because we begin to be possessed by God. There is a third thing: the breaking of bread is the symbol of hospitality, of all that we mean by hearth and home; and so through the bread and wine we are restored also to our roots in the human family, and our individualism is taken away from us, and the loneliness and frustration that come of it.

' And again there is something more. The sacrament of unity is also the sacrament of peace. Have you noticed how it is always the rootless people who are restless, always struggling and scheming for power, for influence, for money? The Eucharist gives us peace precisely because it gives us roots, in this world and the next, in the human family and the divine. Every man wants to have a full life, wants to exercise power and responsibility of one kind or another, wants to be happy; but the restless, rootless man tries to seize upon these things, to win them by domination and domineering, and so power degenerates into tyranny and brutality, and the longing for happiness becomes a ruthless egoism. If we are given great gifts we have to remember that they are indeed God's gifts, to be used for his purposes, in poverty of spirit. If we are given power and authority we have to remember that they must be exercised only in obedience to a greater power and a higher authority, in meekness of heart. If we are given happiness we have to try to accept it humbly from God's hands and make it part of that *caritas* in which we are meant to live. And all this the Church teaches us, again, through the water, the wood, the cup, through the symbolism of sacrifice which shows us that things are made most perfect when they are raised to a higher plane, as when the sensuous becomes the vehicle of spirit, and that they are raised only when they are offered, as bread and wine are offered.

'It does something yet more for us: one final thing. It unites us with all the deepest longings of all the human race: that yearning for rebirth into infinite life which is the burden of mankind's unvarying secular dream. But it does much more than that. It gives us, first a deep and complete understanding of the dream; and then the divine fulfilment of it. As the Mass is offered, this little room becomes filled with God as the upper room where the apostles waited was filled with the Spirit at the first Pentecost; and in that divine presence, if only we let it flood into us and abide in us, all ugliness is exorcized, all unreality transcended, because in it there is the power that, "having marvellously created the world, has still more marvellously redeemed it."

'The Mass is the supreme way to the recovery of Nature, as it is the supreme way to the recovery of God. It is the door through which mankind can pass into the world it has always dreamed of but never attained: the world of the great sanities and sanctities of Nature, the world in which the unity of the human family is achieved, the world, above all, which is God's presence and indwelling, and which alone holds in its stillness the secret of unassailable tranquillity and peace.'

X

The Recovery of Community

IN THE previous chapter we considered in passing the loss of real community in modern life, and the horror of the substitute forms of community. What is the cause of this loss?

For the christian the first and most important answer is obvious. 'Where there is no God, there is no man,' wrote Berdyaev: 'that, we have found by experience.' The brotherhood of man is dependent upon the acceptance of the fatherhood of God. We may recall the words of Dostoevsky quoted in an earlier chapter: 'The roots of our thoughts and feelings are not here but in other worlds, and [if the sense of oneness with those other worlds] grows weak or is destroyed in you, the heavenly growth will die in you. Then you will be indifferent to life or even grow to hate it.' There is no lack today of the hatred of life and of the will-to-death: which is expressed not only in the suicide of individuals but also in race-suicide and in the psychological suicide of the acceptance of totalitarianism of one kind or another, of the diminution or extinction of liberty, independence and initiative.

But there is another obvious enemy of community: the atomization of society which is implicit in the bureaucratic centralization with which we are all too familiar. In proportion as the old organic community dies, man loses his sense of function in the body politic, for in the real sense of the word there is no longer a body: there is only an aggregate of individuals grouped under a remote central authority. 'Individualism has triumphed. If I am a sheer individual, then every other being, every other man especially, is over against me as a menace to me. This is the peculiarity of our society today. . . . The sense of isolation, followed by the sense of menace and of fear, is bound to arise as the feeling of oneness and community with our fellow-men declines, and the feeling of individualism . . . increases. The so-called " cultured " classes are the first to develop . . . individualism, and the first to fall into this state of unconscious menace and fear. The working-classes retain the old blood-warmth of oneness and togetherness some decades longer. Then they lose it, too. And then class-consciousness becomes rampant, and class-hate. . . . Civil strife becomes a necessary condition of self-assertion.'[1]

For the world of tomorrow, this is more than a problem of national death or survival: it is a problem of international death or survival. As the pressure of events leads at last ineluctably to the formation of some sort of central world-authority, there will be every likelihood that the nations will repeat the destructive process followed within the nation by individual human beings: will become themselves in their turn, not members of an organic community, but individualist states still, ranged against each other in fear and therefore in hatred, and therefore in the end calling down upon themselves the dark gods of destruction. But the tragedy of the evolution of human history is that by the time individuals or nations have reached the point of invoking death they are beyond rescue, for ' they know not what they do.'

It is a terrible thing for a man to be a mere cog in an economic machine; it is a far more terrible thing for him to accept his fate. It is a terrible thing to be a mere unit in a political collectivity; but again a far worse thing to accept it. For where there is acceptance there is no remedy. And today there is a very large measure of acceptance—rather, there are today vast numbers of dedicated souls determined to bring about just such a de-humanization of

---

[1] D. H. Lawrence: *Apropos*, pp. 91-2.

It is many years now since Lawrence wrote the above lines; and in the meantime the western world (including ourselves) has moved further and further away from individualism in the nineteenth-century sense of the word—but not in Lawrence's sense of the world. It is indeed one of the striking things about modern totalitarianism, the reaction to that nineteenth-century liberalism, that so far from remedying the evils of the individualism it attacks, it on the contrary intensifies them. The constant purges, the ever-present fear of being found guilty of deviation from the party line, cannot but induce a sense of loneliness, ' menace and fear '; and the destruction of real community is nowhere shown more clearly, or more horribly, than in the denunciations of parents by their children, of husbands by their wives, of friend by friend.

society in the name of the political religion to which they have given their faith. And they will win the day unless, before it is too late, the great mass of men and women can be given back their sense of creative community, their sense of themselves as creative beings, and social beings, and socially-creative beings.

Man is made in the image of God, to be creative in his turn: creative in his work, his love, his home, and creative also in and of community. For he is a social animal in that double sense: that to reach his own full stature he needs community, but also to reach his own full stature he needs to play his part in the creating of community. It is the paradox of man that while on the one hand he is self-subsistent and, in St Thomas's phrase, *perfectissimum in natura*, the highest of earthly creatures, on the other hand he is far from self-sufficient: culturally, economically, politically, he needs others, and needs others not merely individually but in community —not merely for the help others can give him individually to live the good life, but for the help which community as such can give him to live the good life.

The primary human community, which fulfils the deepest needs and most deeply remedies the deficiencies of individual men and women, is the family. This too, as we have seen, is something that has to be made: the love and unity of the man and woman have to be made, the home has to be made, the family has to be made; and again here there is the twofold casuality: the love of the man and woman makes the child, but also the child makes (perfects) the love of the man and woman for each other. And when the primary community is thus made, its continued existence and its growth to perfection depend upon the contributions to the common life made by each member of the family in accordance with the principle of diversity of function. Father and mother have each their different part to play; the children, though dependent on the parents, made by the parents, yet have their own essential contribution to make to the life of the home.

But in many obvious ways the family in its turn is not self-sufficient. Primarily it needs that erosphere we considered before, the *caritas* which alone can guard it from disintegrating elements and lead it to its full fruition. Secondarily it needs the greater human community: it needs the support *of* the common life, it needs *to* support the common life, if it is to attain the true fullness of its own life. But that means in fact that the greater community can be wisely and healthily built only on the principles of the family: for if it is built simply on the principle of society-for-man it must sink back into individualism and the dire effects of individualism, while if it is built simply on the opposite principle of man-for-society it becomes a totalitarian tyranny. Put the two principles together, however, as in the family, and you have neither tyranny nor selfishness but precisely a larger family: a community of free human beings, co-operating freely in the common making of the common life and at the same time reaching their own fulfilment through the benefits conferred on them by the common life.

But the family is more than an exemplar of what the life of the greater community should be: it is as such an organic part of the greater community. A nation which is no more than an atomist aggregate of individuals is doomed to sterility because any form of common creation is (apart perhaps from times of crisis) impossible on so vast a scale, and the way is opened to totalitarianism whether benevolent or otherwise: to a regimented 'welfare state' or to the horrors of modern slavery and forced labour-camps. Where, on the other hand, you have individuals making their own family life, and families making together the life of village or small community, and villages and towns in their turn co-operating in making the life of province or county, and so finally to the life of the nation as a whole: there you have a society which is healthy because organic and because the common life is not a question of conforming to a blue-print imposed from above, but something really growing up from below, something which the community as a whole and not just one section of the community can be said to have created.

This indeed is the christian idea of democracy: not a mob-rule, not the idealization of the Popular Will into a final court of appeal, but the freedom of the individual, within the framework of eternal and natural law and under the authority of a just and representative executive, to help in the moulding of the community life.

Within the framework of law; but also within the vital stream of tradition. The constant emergence of new situations and new needs implies a corresponding constant demand for new forms. The dynamic life-process is formulated and made static in a pattern of law, but as life is always moving and changing so the pattern is in constant need of adaptation; yet to be healthy all such adaptations must themselves be part of tradition, or the current of life will be cut. Tradition means, precisely, a receiving of a heritage and a handing on of the heritage, but a handing on with vital additions, as when the poet of today, living in and nourished by the tradition of English poetry, hands it on to his successors still the English tradition but enriched by his own original contribution to it. Just as there is a false conservatism which will allow no good to be said of anything that is new, so there is a false progressivism which can see nothing good in anything that is old. You cannot adapt if you destroy the past.

How are such adaptations to be made? It is not everybody's vocation to be concerned in political life in the narrow sense; but that does not prevent anybody from playing his part in the common work, for the work is achieved in many ways: here also there is diversity of function. Adaptations can be made directly, through political action; they can be brought about indirectly, through the dissemination of ideas, through books and films and radio, through fashions in literature, in social habits, through the ordinary exchanges of social intercourse: anyone who is himself living a vital, creative life will thereby sooner or later influence his society.

Within the community life the function of the State, the executive, is, in the christian view, not merely negative, not confined to defending the individual or the nation from aggression, nor to the 'hindering of hindrances' to individual freedom of action; it has the positive function of helping individuals to the attainment of the 'good life,' of St Thomas's 'natural beatitude.' And here there is obvious possibility of tensions between the individual and the group, and in particular of encroachments by the State on the freedom of individual and family life. Here the Church's position is quite unequivocal: in the last resort, society is for man and not *vice versa*, and society is for the family and not *vice versa*.

For the christian principles are clear: the human being's ultimate end is God, and the 'supernatural beatitude' of life with God. The means to this end are determined by the eternal law of God and the natural law which is derived from it. Within this ultimate purpose there is the secondary aim: the attainment of natural beatitude through life-in-society; but this latter aim, being secondary, must be regulated by the former. And as it is the individual and the family who are concerned with the ultimate end, not the State, so, as *Rerum Novarum* clearly stated, the State must not absorb the individual or the family: both must be allowed free and untrammelled action so far as is consistent with the common good and the interests of others.

Hence a community as opposed to a collectivity must be based on respect for the basic rights of the individual: the right to live, to found a family, to choose a vocation; the right to liberty of thought and conscience. It must be based on respect for the rights of the family: on the principle that the child belongs to the parents until it is grown up; that the family's home is its castle; that it has the right to such private property as will ensure its own security now and in the future. It is indeed the duty of the State to step in for the good of the child where parents fail in their duty (and they do indeed fail); but the greater danger lies in the other direction, in failing to notice encroachments, or in accepting them as saving trouble and responsibility; for then the creative family life dies, and if that dies, community dies.

In this context, then, there are plenty of dragons to be slain if community life is to survive. There is bureaucratic totalitarianism, which destroys freedom and creativeness; there are all the forms of regimentation, benevolent or otherwise, which achieve tidiness and perhaps efficiency at the expense of personality; there is the growing threat to individual and family rights through State encroachments in general and in particular through the substitution of statute law for the great principles of the common law; there is the increasing tendency to oust the family altogether (and indeed many other small social groupings) by putting the individual more and more under the direct supervision of a central authority; finally, there is the whole trend away from the organic and towards the more and more rigidly organized.

But we shall not achieve much good if we think of all the dragons as external to us. The first step to restoring a creative community is to restore a creative personalism in individuals, in ourselves. If indeed 'individualism has triumphed' and 'men only know one another in menace,' the first thing is to understand exactly what is wrong in this man-to-man relationship, and to remedy it.

What, in the christian view, ought the basis of this relationship to be?

St Thomas Aquinas in the *Summa Theologica*, treats of two virtues, both of which are sometimes called *amicitia* (friendship) though they differ widely. The first is connected with justice: it is a question of affability or friendliness rather than of friendship properly so-called, and is 'a certain natural equity' which obliges a man to 'live agreeably with his fellow-men.'[1] St Thomas is here in fact following Aristotle, whom he quotes repeatedly, in his description of the 'civic virtues' of the magnanimous man.[2] The affable man is neither obsequious, a flatterer, on the one hand, nor surly and contentious on the other; but his affability, which is the mean between these two extremes, will express itself in a willingness to listen courteously to others, to speak cheerfully, to act with urbanity.

But for Aristotle 'the state in question differs from friendship in that it implies no passion or affection for one's associates; since it is not by reason of loving or hating that such a man takes everything in the right way, but by being a man of a certain kind.'[3] For St Thomas the position is radically different: the ways in which affability is expressed may well be the same, but the motive behind them is different; for in the christian life all virtues are to be seen as in-formed, ensouled, by *caritas*. Friendliness, then, cannot be simply a question of external behaviour, of acting always with courtesy because it would be derogatory to the dignity of the subject

---

[1] *Sum. Theol.* IIa IIae. cxiv-cxvi.
[2] *Ethica Nichomachea*, iv, 6.
[3] *op. cit.* (trans. Ross).

to act otherwise. There is an abyss of difference between the aristotelean gentleman and the christian gentleman.

The second virtue which St Thomas treats under the heading of *amicitia* is precisely charity, which he defines in terms of friendship—of friendship and *not* of friendliness.[1] He does not of course hold that the law of love commands us to be friends in the normal sense of the word with all men; but he does hold that the essence of friendship is something that can be true and ought to be true of all human relationships. For essentially friendship means three things. It means willing the good of your friend[2]; it means that such well-wishing must be mutual, and that therefore you must be not only generous enough to give but humble enough to accept; it means finally that there must be *communicatio*, a sharing of life, of ideas, ideals, dreams, labours, joys, sorrows. This threefold relationship is obviously realized most fully in the intimacy of what we call friendship in the ordinary sense; but just as it can be true of the relationship between man and God (in so far as man comes gradually to know and share the mind and the redeeming work of God and, taking humbly from God the gifts he offers, gives them back again in the form of loving service), so it can be true of the relationship between a man and all other men: in so far as he is greathearted enough to will the good of all men, humble enough to accept help from any man, and loving enough to be ready to share the dreams, the needs, the joys and sorrows of any man who comes his way. When you give food to the hungry or drink to the thirsty, or comfort to the afflicted, acting not from a chilly ideal of what is courteous and correct, still less from a sense of condescension, but because you have a real and humble interest in human beings, you fulfil the definition of friendship. The Samaritan was a friend.

Here, then, you have something much deeper than friendliness; but when this spirit in-forms friendliness, as in the christian scheme of things it must; when you have this creative charity in-forming the civic virtue; when you have a courtesy which is not external

---

[1] *Sum. Theol.* IIa IIae, xxiii, 1.

[2] 'In Italian the natural way of expressing love is to say: *ti voglio bene* (I wish you well). I know nothing more moving than this popular expression of affection which corresponds perfectly with the metaphysical definition of love.' (Thibon, *op. cit.* p. 131, n.1.)

and superficial but motived by real love, then you have a power which can move the world, a power which will exorcize the 'menace' and the fear, a power creative of unity between people and between peoples.

What then must *caritas* achieve in us in order to make possible this universal interest and concern? First of all it must keep alive in us a creative mind: open, uninhibited, receptive, and therefore sympathetic to what is new and strange to us. Nothing is easier than to be stupidly intolerant of the different ways of thought and behaviour, the different ideals and principles, of other races and other ages. Nothing is easier, as life goes on, than to sink back into well-worn grooves of thought and prejudice from which there is no emergence, to become set in an intellectual immobility, a hardening of the psychological arteries; so intellectual sympathy becomes impossible, and without that sympathy there is no possibility of understanding, and without understanding there is no well-wishing, and *caritas* becomes an impossibility: you cannot have a house of hospitality in which the windows are for ever shuttered and the doors for ever barred.

The creative mind is of little avail without the creative heart. It is only the two together that can produce community. But for us in this fallen and sin-laden world the creative heart always implies once again the dark journey—but the dark journey seen now, not as the individual's own passage to rebirth in fullness of life, but as his creative sharing in the redemptive journey of the Word made flesh: a going down, with the Word, into the depths, to help there his fellow-men.

In preceding pages we have thought of three different views of the significance of these present times in man's history as a whole: first, the view of those who see the present age as preparing for, or initiating, the age of the Spirit, an age of greater inwardness, of a new flowering of the contemplative spirit, of the spirit of *caritas*; secondly, the view that we are entering upon an age of Mary, in which the influence of the Mother of God, and of all that is implied for us in the figure of the Maiden-Mother, will be far greater than before; finally, the view that in these days God will be discovered anew, transcendent-immanent, the God of pity, dwelling within the sorrows and the squalors of humanity, dwelling within the dark waters out of which the new, divinely-given, life will spring.

But these three views are not in fact different. Symbolically speaking, the water, the spirit, the mother are one: ' Unless a man be born again (from his mother) of water and the spirit . . .' The Spirit, by an inward fecundation, quickens the dark waters, the womb of life, and the earth is renewed. In theology there is a close connection between the Spirit and the Mother: the Spirit is associated with the wisdom of the heart, the wisdom taught by love, by eros the feminine principle; and Mary in her turn is the *Sedes sapientiae*, associated by the Church with that divine wisdom which she embodies: ' Pure effluence of his glory who is God all-powerful, she feels no passing taint; she, the glow that radiates from eternal light, she, the untarnished mirror of God's majesty, she the faithful echo of his goodness. . . .'[1]

But again, the wisdom will never be learnt, the Spirit never accepted, except in the darkness of the night-journey, the darkness of the womb. Always the individual christian comes to the new life by way of his own particular darkness, by taking up his own particular cross and following Christ. If, in a new age, christendom as a whole is to be reborn, if in a new age the world as a whole is to be reborn, what form will the darkness take? It might be a period in which an attempt would be made, on a scale hitherto unknown, to exterminate the Church, a period therefore in which ' the Church would live on obscurely, like a seed in the ground, worshipping no longer in cathedrals but in catacombs, awaiting either the end or a new beginning '[2]; it might be that, as Léon Bloy thought, salvation would come to the west from a reborn Russia, which has always in its theology laid such stress on the doctrine of *kenosis*, of God's self-emptying, on the central importance of the divine Sophia—and, ' for the Orthodox Church, the Blessed Virgin unites in herself the heavenly Wisdom of God and the Wisdom of the created world '[3]—and, finally, on the ideals of

---

[1] *Wisdom*, vii, 25-26.
[2] Guitton: *The Blessed Virgin*, p. 180.
[3] Guitton, *op. cit.* p. 185.

poverty and humiliation. Or, perhaps, it might be that the christian west would itself turn anew to such ideals and to such aspects of the mystery of the Godhead, and so return itself to its sources, and find in its devotion to the Mother of God and of men, today so deep and so widespread, these other aspects, expressed in terms of the Spirit and the water, which will in fact lead it down into the recreative depths.

For if once the christian world were in fact to discover God anew, really to discover him, not with the mind alone but with the heart, immanent and suffering in the stresses and tragedy of modern life, there would be no further question, there could be no further question, about the coming of an age of the Spirit: it would have come. To discover such a God is to discover the Fire, and to become incandescent with the heat of the Fire.

‘ “ You think that all this . . . all the pain of the world, was Christ's cross? ”

“ God's cross,” said Thibault. “ And it goes on.”

“ The Patripassian heresy,” muttered Abelard mechanically. “ But, oh God, if it were true. Thibault, it must be. At least, there is something at the back of it that is true. And if we could find it—it would bring back the whole world.” ’[1]

It *is* true, essentially; and we *can* find it[2]; but to find it fully and bring back the world with it, we should have to find it not, again, with our minds only but in the depths of our hearts. And having found it we should also have found, among other things, the way back to community. ‘ The *Supper*,’ to use a phrase of Prof. Guitton's, ‘ has superseded the *Symposium* of a preparatory age in which the essential factor was omitted.’[3] The impersonal or condescending bestowal of ‘ social welfare ’ is as remote from real community as is Aristotle's ‘ affable man.’ What the modern western world needs, but cannot even understand, is the *baiser au lépreux*. ‘ And when supper was done . . . he riseth . . . and layeth aside his garments, and having taken a towel, girded himself.

[1] Helen Waddell: *Peter Abelard* (1939 edit.), pp. 290-291.
[2] I have attempted to show that this is so, and incidentally that Thibault's view is *not* the Patripassian heresy, in *The Pain of Christ*, ch. vii.
[3] Guitton: *Essay on Human Love*, p. 198.

After that, he putteth water into a basin, and began to wash the feet of the disciples, and to wipe them with the towel wherewith he was girded.'[1]

Whatever the future may hold for the Church and for the world it is for us to try as best we can to prepare for an age of the Spirit, the Mother, the Water: to live as best we can our own dark journey, to deepen as best we can the sense of our own sin, our own impotence and incompetence; to pray as best we can the prayer of the Publican, Lord, be merciful to me a sinner, seeing ourselves as 'stripped and poor and naked' before God; to understand with our hearts the descent into the dark waters, to know in our hearts the finding, in humanity's sins and sorrows, of the redemptive God; and so through all this to learn the lesson of inwardness and stillness, of depth, of sorrow and wisdom, of *caritas* as the erosphere in which alone the soul can breathe and grow; and so, having found for ourselves at least the beginnings of the road to renewal, to find also the way to the recovery of community, the beginning of the re-establishment of the human peoples as a human family under the all-embracing fatherhood of God, hoping, praying and working for the day when the fatherhood will at last be universally acknowledged, the brotherhood universally achieved, and the words of St Paul universally verified: ' You are all the children of God by faith in Christ Jesus, for as many of you as have been baptized in Christ have put on Christ. There is neither Jew nor Greek: there is neither bond nor free: there is neither male nor female: for you are all one in Christ Jesus.'

[1] *John*, xiii, 2-5.

XI

The Redemption of Matter

THE STORY of mankind begins in a garden; and all through that story the beauty of Nature, of God's creatures, has been meant to give and has given joy to men's hearts. So too have the works of man's own hands: the beauty to be found in good tables and chairs, in fine glassware and silver, in well-seasoned timber, in warm mellow brick or the cool dignity of stone. All these things help to make the world what it should be, a pleasant place to live in. But as we have seen, they are meant to do more than that: ' from the foundations of the world men have caught sight of [God's] invisible nature, his eternal power and his divineness, as they are known through his creatures '[1]: man is meant to learn something of the love of God from the loveliness of material things.

But as we know all too well, there is another side to the story. Stupidity, hatred, wickedness, destroy the beauty that God has made, destroy the beauty that man himself has made, and give us instead the world of greed and ugliness and desolation: the atom-bomb, the slum, the slag-heap, the noise, the dirt. And nowadays it seems that material things are abused and defiled, on a scale never known before, so as to drag down man himself and destroy him.

This is a cruel world, and through the ages men have killed and tortured each other; but today science is used to destroy—through torture, through drugs, through a perversion of psychiatry—not men's bodies merely but their minds and wills and personalities.

[1] *Romans*, i, 20.

173

This is a sinful world, and through the ages men have sinned with their bodies; but today again the bodily love of men and women for each other has been cheapened and commercialized in a way never known before. Human beings are partly body and partly spirit; and we know all too well how constantly the two elements are at war with each other; but that constant struggle is only a part of a much larger one, in which the whole of the material side of life, instead of joining in the praise of God and making life lovely, seems to be moving further and further away from God, to be making life more and more ugly, and to be dragging man down more and more rapidly into defilement and evil.

In the *Apocalypse* there is a description of a wonderful and mysterious vision which seems to put all this into a very vivid picture for us. Two great signs, we are told, appeared in the heavens. The first was ' a woman that wore the sun for her mantle, with the moon under her feet, and a crown of twelve stars about her head '; and ' she bore a son, the son who is to herd the nations like sheep.' The second portent is a great dragon, ' fiery-red, with seven heads and ten horns, and on each of the seven heads a royal diadem; his tail dragged down a third part of the stars in heaven, and flung them to earth. And he stood fronting the woman who was in child-birth, waiting to swallow up the child.' And then, the vision goes on, ' fierce war broke out in heaven, where Michael and his angels fought against the dragon. The dragon and his angels fought on their part but could not win the day or stand their ground any longer; the great dragon, serpent of the primal age, was flung down to earth; he whom we call the devil, or Satan, the whole world's seducer, flung down to earth and his angels with him.' And so, finally, ' in his spite against the woman, the dragon went elsewhere to make war on the rest of her children. . . . And he stood there waiting on the sea beach.'[1]

Now the woman in the vision has been identified by Biblical scholars with Israel bringing forth Christ, or with the Church of Christ; and in a secondary way she has also been identified with our Lady, though some of the details of the vision make it clear that it cannot be to her that the passage immediately refers. But it

[1] *Apocalypse*, ch. xii.

is in any case clear that the woman and her children, attacked by Satan, the mystery of iniquity, and defended by Michael the archangel, represent the world which is the object of God's redeeming love. But the symbolism of sun and moon and stars makes us think of the woman as a figure of dazzling splendour, raised high in glory and majesty, in contrast with the angry fire-red of the dragon crouching on the sands of the sea. And it is the *body* of the woman that is thus made glorious and shining, so that we could think of her here as symbolizing all the physical and material side of life made glorious through redemption—so sharp a contrast, this glory, to the slums we make of our cities, the slums we make of our lives. And so the vision can have for us a special relevance to that glorifying of Mary, the apotheosis of purely human flesh and blood, which we call the Assumption, the doctrine which, after so many centuries, was recently defined by Rome to be part of the christian faith.

And perhaps the foregoing line of thought suggests a reason why this doctrine should be defined at this particular moment in the world's history. The gulf between matter and spirit, between material things and the praise of God, is widening at a pace and to an extent hitherto unknown: it would be very easy nowadays to despair. It would be very easy to despair of this civilization of ours; very easy to despair of the future of our race; very easy to feel that, so far from marching triumphantly forward to a golden age, we are rushing headlong into an abyss; very easy to feel that our world is doomed because all the physical and material side of life must continue to drag man down and degrade him till the heavens are closed to him. But it is just at this moment that the voice of the Church comes to us like a challenge: we are on the contrary to shout aloud our belief in the dignity and holiness of material things; we are to affirm our faith and our hope in the future of man's flesh. The woman who stands in the heavens, the Mother of God, is also the mother of men; and her glory is the guarantee of theirs.

That is why this definition is far from having a purely domestic interest or importance. The greatest definitions have always been defensive: defensive of some more central truth which would

otherwise have been endangered; and it might be asked what was
being defended here, what doctrine was endangered here. But the
Church is not concerned merely with the guarding and defending
of her own children: she is concerned with the guarding and
defending of the whole world. The doctrine of the Assumption
is of supreme importance not merely to catholics but to all men
and women because it means that there is still in the world, there
will always be in the world, a voice to affirm and a power to defend
the dignity and the ultimate glory of matter, of material things, of
human flesh and blood, of the lovely mystery of human love, of
the beauty which is in the work of men's hands. There is a voice
which affirms, there is a power which defends, all the material
things which make life worth while; and they bid us be of good
heart because we can hope in the end to achieve our own lives,
full, rich, deep, unified, free, not by escaping from the flesh and
material things, but by the healing and sanctifying of the flesh and
material things.

And so the voice of the Church is a challenge in another sense:
a challenge not merely to faith and to hope, but to action. In our
own individual lives, in our immediate surroundings, in our social
and political life, there is work to be done, and done quickly. In
politics and economics, in education, in marriage, in the arts and
the sciences, in all our daily life, in all our judgments about the
relative values of this and that, in all our private thoughts and
dreams and actions, there is always the same question to be asked:
Is this thing going to degrade man yet further, for if so we must
fight against it; or is it going to help to build up that oneness of
body and soul, of material things and spiritual things, which in the
end will make possible the assumption of man into the heaven
of God?

In the greatest of the Church's definitions of doctrine concerning
our Lady, the doctrine that she is the mother of God, it was her
Son that the Church was defending. But she is also the mother of
all men; and here, in this doctrine of her Assumption, it is *all* her
sons that the Church is defending. Just as the figure of motherhood is at the very centre of the earthly history of every human
soul, of the earthly history of the human race, so the figure of this

Maiden-Mother is at the very centre of the eternal history of individuals and of the race. If she is attacked, later on her Son will be attacked, and in the end her other children will be attacked. Men will begin by denying some part of her God-given greatness and glory; they will go on sooner or later to deny the divinity of her Son; and in the end there will be no defence for the greatness of humanity itself. In our own history we have seen it happen: we have seen how, first, men tried to dethrone her; and how then they lost faith in her Son, and how, finally, they have lost faith in themselves. The Church's voice is a challenge because, while it tells us to hope because in Mary the flesh is sanctified and glorified, material things are sanctified and glorified, it also tells us to beware because the dragon, defeated, ' went elsewhere to make war on the rest of her children. . . . And he stood there waiting on the sea beach.'

The redemption of matter is not something done for us but something to be done by us, and the immensity of the task is all too obvious. The world of tomorrow will no doubt be characterized by a yet greater, and always increasing, technical power, and the greater the power, the greater the possibilities of degradation, unless meanwhile we can achieve that radical change of heart which would make such degradation impossible. It is once again a question of relearning the lesson of wonder and reverence, and of seeing it as something not merely of æsthetic but of theological importance. The abolition of ugliness is of theological importance because the human personality will not easily grow to its full stature in an environment of ugliness and squalor. It is of theological importance to restore to man the dignity of labour by restoring labour itself from the idea of a money-gaining drudgery to that of a creative vocation. It is of theological importance to fight against the degradation of language (the jargon of the bureaucrat, the vulgarity of a type of journalism); against the degradation of the arts (the sordid advertisements, the commercializing of sex); against the degradation of music, of building, of politics, of conversation, of social manners and customs: because in all these cases you are fighting for the dignity of human flesh and blood and therefore answering the challenge of the Church's definition. The same is still more obviously true, and the task still more obviously urgent, when it is a question of the great issues of social justice, of the abolition of penury and want, of education and culture in general, of marriage and sex, of labour camps and political regimentation. Again, the movement within the Church to restore the purity of its worship and to free it from vulgarities and sentimentalities and squalid bric-à-brac is of theological and not merely of æsthetic importance.[1] And finally the same is true when you come to those personal ideals for which christianity stands but which are nowadays often treated with contempt: the qualities which restore something of the original harmony between flesh and spirit: the moderation and self-control, the purity and gentleness, the graciousness and candour, the simplicity and single-mindedness, the cleanness of heart to which is promised the vision of God.

But again, the work demands of us a radical change of heart. The æsthete, the dilettante, secure in his ivory tower, will never help to redeem matter, for he is concerned only to use it for his own ends, ignoring the degradation of the world outside. The way to wisdom is humility and pity. We shall redeem matter only if with the sense of wonder and reverence and the knowledge which is born of them there goes the humility which is born of the consciousness that it is we who have degraded matter and that if we

[1] We have much here to be thankful for; in contemporary church-building for instance which not only shows an admirable asceticism in its art, an insistence on essentials, on the idea of the church as a temple of sacrifice and not a repository of ecclesiastical *objets*, but also is admirable in its use of contemporary idiom, underlying the Church's actuality instead of presenting it as something outmoded and moribund by attempting to resurrect for it styles which have long since ceased to be an expression of a living culture.

But it is tragic that where language is concerned we should lag so far behind building and the other arts, and find ourselves, where the use of the vernacular is concerned, still bogged down in an ecclesiastical jargon which becomes more and more meaningless as the years go by, and which hides the great realities of faith and of worship under a mass of unreal and ugly verbiage. The prayers, usually called ' devotions,' which say in thirty lines of bad English what could well be said in three, are in fact no aid to devotion; and the uncouth latinisms which are our common currency only make the realities they stand for seem remote from our everyday existence and to that extent meaningless. Why should we allow the loveliness of the litany of our Lady to be sullied by such monstrosities of language as ' Mother Inviolate' and ' Singular Vessel of Devotion'? Why, in the rosary, should we say annunciation when we mean announcement and visitation when we mean visit, as though to rob these events of any relationship to our own lives and desires and needs? (It is something to be thankful for that we do speak of the *Finding* in the Temple and do not repeat the imbecility of the ' Invention of the True Cross'—surely the most infelicitous of all possible mistranslations, and the perfect invitation to what the theologians call the *irrisio infidelium* . . .)

are in fact to redeem it it can only be because God in his pity has come down into our squalors to share them and to bring us renewal through that sharing. The story of the as yet unfallen world begins in a garden; it is to another garden we must go to understand how the subsequent fall is to be repaired.

'And now, with his disciples, he went out across the Cedron valley. Here there was a garden, into which he and his disciples went.'[1] A garden is a symbol of all that we mean by the loveliness of Nature made yet more lovely by human art, and made more warmly and deeply human also by human love: 'My bride, my true love, a close garden, hedged all about, a spring shut in and sealed . . . North wind, awake; wind of the south, awake and come; blow through this garden of mine, and set its fragrance all astir.'[2] Later on in this story of Christ's Passion, at the climax of the scene in the garden, there is another symbol, a kiss, the immediate image and expression of human love; and then, in the high-priest's courtyard, Peter warms himself at the fire and you think of the symbol of the hearth's welcome, the warmth of home; and then finally the story ends with the tree, the wood of life, the womb of life, and his mother and his friend are with him there.

These things, the human, homely things, are images for us of what life ought to be; but here in this story they are incidents set against a very different background. He is dragged from the garden into the dusty, teeming, hostile city, and thence to Golgotha, the hill of skulls; he is dragged from the little circle of friends to be exposed to the howling mob; the tree of life is his tree of death; the kiss is for him the traitor's kiss; and when all is over, the sun, the fiery life-bringer, is darkened and there is darkness over all the earth. So through the ages the two contrasting worlds confront one another: the world of beauty, of the homely things, of life and love; and the world of ugliness, of greed, of darkness and hatred; and the second world attempts to destroy the first. So through the ages war destroys the smiling valley and the hearths lie grey and dead; so evil destroys the human soul and the heart lies dead; and humanity itself turns the tree of life into a tree of death.

[1] *John*, xviii, 1.   [2] *Song of Songs*, iv, 12, 16.

Yet as the story approaches its climax there is one phrase which has a special poignancy for us. It is Christ's prayer for his executioners: Father, forgive them: they know not what they do. As life goes on one comes to realize more and more how true this is, not only of these men, but of all men. Sometimes of course we know all too well what we do: we act as we do because we are what we are: and what we are is the result very largely of the use we have made of our freedom to act as we will. But there is another side to the story. We are what we are, also, to a large extent because of other things, outside our control; because of the bodies our parents gave us, our heredity in general, our environment, the experiences and accidents and influences that come our way in childhood. These things and their effects can lie outside our conscious awareness; when we act we may be acting because of them, our actions determined by them but we unable to see what moves us; we may not understand what we are doing. And so many of the foibles and vices of men seem to be of this sort: there is free will, yes, and if they had been shown these things and had understood them early enough, they might have controlled their destiny better; but there comes a time when it seems that, short of a miracle, it is too late: the mould is set; they will never escape because they will never understand; and so perhaps they will even want to crucify God.

This is true of individual human beings: is it perhaps true also of the world as a whole? St Luke in his Gospel speaks of ' men's hearts withering away within them for fear, as they await the troubles that are overtaking the whole world ': it is an apt enough description of the world of today with its atmosphere of impending doom, as though mankind were convinced that disaster must come and cannot be averted. They know not what they do: is there a parallel between the blind conditioning that lies behind so much of our individual lives and the blind ineluctable march of world events? Must the darkness conquer? Must the hearts of men be killed, the world of men be laid waste, because of our blindness? Or is it rather that we fail to redeem the time, we fail to cure ourselves, we fail to cure the world, because in both cases alike we set about the task in exactly the wrong way? This story of God in the garden seems to tell us that we do.

The tree of death is also the tree of life; the tomb of death is the womb of life; it is through going down with Christ into his death that we are to be ourselves reborn; the dry bones shall live again because the Lord will send his Spirit into the bones: the rebirth is made possible through water and the holy Spirit. Life, in other words, must come from without, from God; but at the same time man must be able to receive it: there are conditions to be fulfilled on his side and it is these that are expressed in terms of going down into the darkness, into the dark waters, into death. For in death and darkness man can be freed from his pride and learn to be humble of heart: he can imitate the Word who ' dispossessed himself and took the nature of a slave ' and then ' lowered [even] his own [human] dignity, accepted an obedience which brought him to death, death on a cross.' And that is why, St Paul goes on, that is why ' God has raised him to such a height, given him a name which is greater than any other name ': that is why: because of his self-humbling even to death.

Everywhere the spectacle confronts us of the destruction of what makes life worth living: man's garden is laid waste, the beauty he has made is ravaged, his home is destroyed, his hearth a heap of dead ashes; and these things are images of a much deeper tragedy, the death that is in his soul. And the dry bones, it is clear, will never find life again of themselves, from within themselves. A dead heart can live again only if the two conditions are fulfilled, a dying world can live again only if the two conditions are fulfilled: if life is brought them from without, and if they themselves are able to receive it. But to be able to receive it they must first admit their own death; and human nature finds that very difficult to do. Men will sometimes say that God is dead; they will very seldom admit that they themselves are dead; and if they do, it is all too often, like Judas, only with the sterile voice of despair.

At the beginning of this chapter we thought of that other garden in which humanity's story begins. In that garden, the symbol of the life we might have had, the life we long for but have lost, there is a tree of life and a tree of knowledge: but man would not *receive* life, he wanted to seize it for himself, dominate over it; he would not *receive* knowledge of the truth, he wanted to fashion it for himself; and so the life is lost; man is expelled from the garden, and his soul dies. His soul dies because he wanted in his pride to make himself God; he tried to take to himself a glory that was not his. But now there is hope for him again because the Son of God did exactly the opposite: he dispossessed himself of the glory that *was* his and became a slave; and so in him humanity was healed, and in him we may each of us be healed, provided only that we in our turn do the same thing, reverse in the same way the primal sin, become humble enough to admit the death that is in us, the evil that is in us, and so, in that act of going down into the darkness where pride is killed, find again the light that is life.

The story of the second Eve reverses the story of the first; and always the key to the reversal lies in the words of Mary: ' Behold the handmaid of the Lord.' To Adam and Eve there comes the serpent tempting, the dragon of the *Apocalypse*; to Mary there comes the angel of the Lord. The serpent is concerned to make them rebel: ' Why hath God commanded you . . . ? ' The angel announces God's will, which Mary will accept whatever it may be. The serpent says, ' You shall be as gods,' and so they lose that presence of God in which they had walked; the angel says, ' The Lord is with thee,' because Mary has accepted the presence wholly. Mary is childlike in the simplicity of her acceptance; Eve is childish in her exaggeration of the divine command—that they were not even to touch the tree—and in her attempt to shift the blame from herself: ' The serpent deceived me.' For Eve the tree is delightful to behold, and she does not see beyond the superficial appeal of independence to the nakedness and the emptiness, the loss of God; for Mary the tree will mean the seven swords, but she does not oppose God's will, she does sense that beyond the death there will be the life. Eve is fascinated by the promise of an impossible knowledge—' Your eyes shall be opened and you shall be as gods ' —and the story goes on to tell, with that irony which so often in the Scriptures veils the pity of God, that their eyes *were* opened— and all that they beheld was their own nakedness. Mary asks no more than the one necessary question, 'How shall this thing be?' —and for the rest, she 'kept all these words,' humbly and quietly 'pondering them in her heart' and so became the image of the divine wisdom. They saw that they were naked, and they hid themselves: the joy and glory of an integrated passion no longer possible to them, for the harmony was destroyed and in this as in everything else they now knew evil, the ugliness that henceforth will corrupt love and loveliness; but Mary, whose heart knows no evil, is in a very different sense 'stripped and poor and naked' before God: hiding nothing from God because there is nothing in her that is not God's. Instead of the pride, the humility; instead of the rebellion, the acceptance; and so, while the serpent is told, 'Cursed art thou among all cattle,' Mary is saluted by the angel as 'Blessed among women.' And while Eve is told, 'In sorrow shalt thou bring forth children,' Mary is told, 'The holy Spirit will come upon thee, and the power of the most High will overshadow thee'—'Wind of the south, awake and come: blow through this garden of mine, and set its fragrance all astir.'

'He is not worthy of me,' Christ said, 'that does not take up his cross and follow me.' The cross is the tree where pride and egoism die; the following is into the tomb where pride and egoism die, and which is therefore the womb of life. 'Do what you are doing now,' wrote de Caussade, 'suffer what you are suffering now; to do all this with holiness'—in other words, to turn death into the fullness of life—'nothing need be changed but your hearts. . . . Sanctity consists in *willing* what happens to us by God's order. . . . Let us love God's will and by means of that love alone, everything in us will become divine.'[1] To will to put back your life into greater hands than yours; to know in your heart your need of a Saviour; to know that otherwise the evil will grow in you, the egoism will grow in you, and destroy you; to know that the only expression of hope for you is the prayer of the Publican, 'O Lord, be merciful to me, a sinner'; to pray to God with John Donne to batter your rebellious heart till it is liberated; to remember always the words spoken to the *Staretz* Silouan: 'Keep thy mind in hell, and despair not'; to know in one's bones that it is no idle

[1] J. P. de Caussade: *Self-Abandonment to Divine Providence*, ch. i, 9.

rhetoric to say that 'there is no health in us'; these are the cross and the tomb that lead to life—and these are the things that alone will make the world of tomorrow saner and healthier and happier than the world of yesterday and today.

'In all the possibility of things,' said William Law, 'there is and can be but one happiness and one misery. The one misery is nature and creature left to itself, the one happiness is the Life, the Light, the Spirit of God, manifested in nature and creature. That is the true meaning of the word of our Lord: There is but one that is good, and that is God.' 'As long as I am this or that or have this or that,' wrote Eckhart, 'I am not all things and I have not all things. Become pure till you neither are nor have either this or that; then you are omnipresent and, being neither this nor that, are all things.' There is the same lesson in the cry of St Catherine of Genoa: 'My Me is God, nor do I recognize any other Me except my God himself'; in the figure of the meek little old hermit in Russia who allows himself to be rudely treated by his servant but says of himself with tears, 'I am not humble, I am arrogant: I want a place in the heavenly kingdom'; or again in the words of the eastern mystic: 'Would you become a pilgrim on the road of Love? The first condition is that you make yourself humble as dust and ashes.'

Let us go back into the garden where Christ began his final dark journey: go back, away from the noise and tumult, the sin and squalor, of the city; back into the garden where he takes the cup that is offered him to drink. Everything is silent and still; no sound but the beat of wings. In the silence of night he was born into life; in the silence of the night he was born into the death that brings life; for us too it is the first condition—we never learn life, we never learn wisdom, unless we learn to be still. But then secondly there is the clash of desires in Christ, and the consummation of the struggle in loving surrender to his destiny: Not my will but thine be done; and so for us too, sanctity 'consists in willing what happens to us by God's order.' But then thirdly, out of that death of self-will there comes the birth of new life, of new power: 'when he said to them, I am Jesus of Nazareth,' St John tells us, 'they all shrank back, and fell to the ground.' But this is not power as the world knows power, for his kingship is not of this world. Heaven, said Lao-Tzu, 'arms with *pity* those whom it would not see destroyed.' This is the power which will command, Feed my sheep, untidy, mangy, though they are; it is the power which will reserve its human breath to pray, Father, forgive them, they know not what they do. Out of the stillness the acceptance; out of the acceptance the power; out of the power the life-giving pity.

And so that divine prayer comes to us now with a new accent, a new meaning. Often we do not understand our own actions, our own motives—and it is because our vision is so narrow, we have so little sight of God, and therefore so little knowledge of ourselves. What is it to see stars and galaxies and solar systems which to earlier ages were unimaginable unless we somehow glimpse the Love that moves the sun and the other stars? And unless we know Love, how shall we know ourselves? For we never find ourselves at all unless we learn that our name too is love. But to learn to be still, and love God's will, and go back with Christ to the garden and to the tree; to say, as Christ said on the tree, Father, into *thy* hands I commend my spirit: this is in the end to become infallible. You are infallible then because you are identified with love; you are infallible because you live then, not you, but Christ lives in you; you are infallible as all the poor and simple and illiterate lovers of God are infallible; for where there are knowledge, brilliance, power without love, there is pride the death-bringer; but to the poor in spirit is promised the kingdom, the meek shall possess the land, and it is the clean of heart who see God.

We know not what we do: and what then *are* we to do? The wise men tell us, Just the one thing: recognize and accept your ignorance, and give it into God's keeping. Love is grown cold in us, and how then *are* we to love? The wise men tell us, Just the one thing: recognize and accept your emptiness, and give that into God's keeping. For if you once admit in your heart to God that whether the evil you do is entirely to your blame or not, whether you understand what you do or not, whether you are learned or illiterate, brilliant or stupid, strong or weak, great or lowly, still in either case before God you are poor and naked, then the Spirit can flow into you, the dry bones can live again, the fountains of

water can spring up into life everlasting, and through you the face
of the earth can be renewed.

But there is something more. In the Middle Ages there was a
legend that it was on the hill of Golgotha that Adam was buried,
and that out of his tomb grew the tree on which God hung. Adam
is humanity, once glorious and now fallen; Christ is the new
Adam, the new humanity, which was fallen but is now through
him made glorious again, rising out of the grave of the old. When
Christ took the cup he was strengthened in power; but it was the
power that brings life through pity; and whenever a man takes
the cup in company with him he too is made strong in the same
power, and the power goes forth from him despite himself, and
through him the nations are healed, the world is renewed, matter
is redeemed and sanctified.

We can say if we will that our world is dying, the material
world is degraded and destroyed, because of the malice of men who
know not what they do; but if so, let us say also that our world
will be born again and matter be redeemed through the love of
men who also know not what they do because their concern is not
to do great things in the world but only to love the world greatly.
It is they who will dig and plant anew the garden and the vineyard;
it is they who, being humble and reverent before God's creation,
will renew it; it is they who will rekindle the fire in the
hearth and bring back to men's hearts the warmth and tenderness
of love.

And so the words of our Lord are a challenge to us because of
what he also said: 'He that is not with me is against me.' We
cannot be neutral: we must be on the side of life or the side of
death; we must either carry forward his work or oppose it. But
how can we be on the side of life if in our weakness and our squalor
we are steeped in sin, steeped in death? 'He saved others,' they
cried out at him in mockery: 'himself he cannot save'; but it
was the voice of death that spoke in them, and the voice of life
speaks differently. If at least we come before God in nothingness,
if at least we recognize and accept our worthlessness, if at least we
pray always the prayer, Thou who art all Fire, have mercy on me;
then perhaps we ought to hope that, if we love the world enough

to want to save it, we may in the end hear the words reversed for us: 'They saved others because they loved them; and so in spite of their ignorance and their folly, their waywardness and weakness, their cowardice and their denials, they too shall be saved: for their name is love, and Love is *my* name.'

Acknowledgments

The author and publishers wish to express their thanks to the following for permission to include in this book passages from works in which they hold the copyright: the author and P. J. Kenedy & Sons, for the passages from *Essay on Human Love* and *The Blessed Virgin* by Jean Guitton on pages 22, 125, 127, 136–7, 138, 143, 147–8, 170, 171–2; the author and Harper & Brothers for the passages from *The Perennial Philosophy* by Aldous Huxley on pages 19–20, 24–5; Dodd, Mead & Co. for the passages from *Psychology of the Unconscious* and *Contributions to Analytical Psychology* by Dr. C. G. Jung on pages 63–4, 80–1, 82–3, 91–3, 106, 121, 134–5, 136; Henry Holt & Co. for the passages from *The Desert Fathers*, *Peter Abelard*, and *The Wandering Scholars* by Helen Waddell on pages 9, 66, 71 and 171; The Newman Press for the passages from *The Complete Works of St. John of the Cross* translated by E. Allison Peers on pages 85–6, 100, and 101; New Directions for the passages from *Seeds of Contemplation* by Thomas Merton on pages 65 and 114; Twayne Publishers, Inc. for the passages from *Apropos of Lady Chatterley's Lover* by D. H. Lawrence on pages 12, 16, 161–2; the author and Henry Regnery Company for the passages from *The World of Silence* by Max Picard on pages 9–10, 44–5; the author and Pantheon Books, Inc. for the passages from *Leisure the Basis of Culture* by Joseph Pieper on pages 11, 26, 30, 36; the author and Henry Regnery Company for the passages from *What God Has Joined Together* by Gustave Thibon on pages 117–8, 120, 121, 135; E. P. Dutton & Co., Inc. for the passages from *Mysticism* and *The Mystic Way* by Evelyn Underhill on pages 19, 27–8, 34–5, 84–5, 87–8, 93; the author and Henry Regnery Company for the passages from *God and the Unconscious* by Fr. Victor White on pages 53, 57, 59, 65, 110.

DATE DUE

GAYLORD			PRINTED IN U.S.A.